One Simple Thing That Changes

Everything in Your Business

How Smart Real Estate and Sales Professionals Think and Grow Rich While Making a Difference

Beverly Boston

Author, Master Business Coach, Trainer and Mentor

"I had no idea that being your authentic self could make me as rich as I've become. If I had, I'd have done it a lot earlier."

~ Oprah Winfrey

ISBN: 1478385073
ISBN-13: 978-1478385073

DEDICATION

This book is dedicated to small thinking.
May it rest in peace!

CONTENTS

INTRODUCTION

It starts with a daring, big dream.

It takes courage and confidence, to live like you mean it and if you're reading this I know you've got what it takes, and you do too.

Don't take my word for it. Think about all the times you have found out that you really can achieve what you set out to do. Yet, keep in mind how anxious you were going into that apparently impossible challenge. Despite the uncertain steps, you did it, you believed in yourself, and said, "Ha, that wasn't so bad, what's next?" Or did you hold yourself back in your comfortable place once again and praise yourself for continuing to play it safe?

Every successful realtor and sales professional I've ever talked to or worked with tells me that the biggest secret to their success has been daring to dream big dreams, planning for the long haul, and keeping the momentum going and moving forward. The One Simple Thing of daring to dream big dreams has had the biggest impact on their business growth and helping more people.

As you tackle the challenge of this journey, be honest with yourself, do the work, and be bold!

Let me be the first to say, welcome to the Smart Thinkers Club, my friend.

Let's get started!

Beverly Boston
Master Real Estate, Business Coach & Mentor

—

FORWARD

Beverly Boston has accomplished it! This book has the power to transform your business and your life. Through her studies of mindset, behavior and thinking, Beverly has come across the simple, yet profound formula to utilize bigger and better thinking, and daring to dream bigger by using the power of the right questions. This book will show you the way to use your mind and values in achieving what is most important to you.

Through Beverly's simple formula she will show how to focus your thinking like never before. The outcome will be that you will tap into hidden strengths within you, find the best answers to your greatest challenges, stop hiding out and thinking small, and bridge the gap from where you currently are to achieving your biggest and most daring dreams and goals.

The speed of business today is too frantic for many entrepreneurs, like being on a train that won't stop. They are working longer hours, anxious about their futures, coping with finances, and trying to keep up with huge amounts of information flooding them daily. Numerous sales professionals carry an enormous amount of guilt because they feel unsuccessful, unseen, unheard and are unhappy—dissatisfied with their businesses. They are asking themselves: is this all there is?

Can you relate to this? There is an increasing need for business owners to take back control. One Simple Thing That Will Change Everything in Your Business will help you do that in numerous ways. And the benefits apply whether you are a real estate agent, executive, sales professional, or a multi- millionaire.

The better questions you ask, the better your business will become. This book helps you to stop being held hostage to small thinking and asking the wrong questions and thinking small. She has given you the formula to unlock the business that you always wanted and dare to dream big.

Daring to dream big is not about looking outside yourself for something that you don't have; Beverly shows you how to reach inside to find what is already there. Your degree of personal fulfillment, abundance, success, and wealth can be linked back to the right questions you ask and the actions you take that Beverly has suggested.

Beverly Boston has mentored and coached thousands of entrepreneurs helping them tap in to their daring big dreams to succeed on their own terms. And she will teach you that anything is possible...if you dare to dream big!

Succeeding on my own terms and the success I have enjoyed can be linked back to the right questions I have asked from this book. I have dreamed big and asked big questions, which have resulted in unending success, joy, happiness and freedom. You can too, by asking the right questions found in One Simple Thing That Changes Everything in Your Business.

Sylvia Nicholson

Human Resources Manager
www.labinal.com

One Simple Thing that Changes Everything in Your Business

Dare to do something SO big you can't believe you're doing it!

"As you become clearer about who you really are, you'll be better able to decide what is best for you - the first time around."
~ Oprah Winfrey

Oprah, a woman whom we all watch and listen to with enormous interest, says that her success in business has mostly been the result of her ability to focus on the big picture, and her long-term goals. Even with all of her success, she continues to dare to dream big dreams when creating the next chapter in her life and business—bringing together the right mix of people and the right opportunities that can make them happen.

"When change is unavoidable," says Oprah, "you must recognize it, embrace it, and discover ways to make it work for you." That's invaluable advice from someone who dares to dreams big dreams and has literally changed the world as a result. Oprah is a good example of someone who uses the One Simple Thing again and again during her business growth, and very successfully.

Of course, it can be daunting to compare our own businesses to that of someone like Oprah. You might say to yourself that she was the right person in the right place at the right time in her career that she got the lucky breaks, or that no one will ever again be successful entirely like she has been successful.

When comparing money in the bank that could very well be true. But while Oprah may have a distinctive position in the business world, there is also a distinctive position in the world for you—you just have to discover it.

When I speak of dreaming, I'm not speaking about daydreaming. The kind of dreaming I'm speaking about also requires doing. You dare to dream your big dream and you start to make it come true; you write it down and share it with the people around you. You begin to plan your path and look for likeminded people who can assist you along the way, you breathe some life into it, keep fanning the flames that will make it brighter and keep in mind that all that you do, say, or think is important.

I myself have dared to dream big dreams and a lot of them have come true as a result. When applying the One Simple Thing in my own business it takes me from what could happen to what will happen successfully.

For instance, I know that I will write several books, this being the first of this length, and many more to come. I know that I will have bestselling books on the top New York Times bestsellers list, and they will remain at the top of the list for years.

I continue to dream, reaching out a bit more, taking deliberate risks, knowing that if I've risen this far—and the view has been extraordinary—then I can surely persist to rise higher and higher.

Every dream I have achieved has taken me one step closer to the big vision I have for my business and life.

As sales professionals we thrive on achievement and the bigger we dare to dream, the more we can achieve to make the world a much better place for all. Those who dare to dream big dreams are the only ones who will achieve big dreams.

You may have heard of Jim Carrey. Jim Carrey was once a stand-up comic performing in comedy clubs across North America who dreamed of worldwide stardom. Following his celebrated success in a series of several movies I saw him interviewed on Oprah. In the interview, he talked about his struggle to be successful at the start of his career, the long nights on the road, and how six or seven years previously he had written a check to himself for $10 million dollars and dated it October 1995. In 1995, Jim Carrey signed a contract to start in a sequel to one of his movies for $10 million dollars. Shortly afterward, he received a record sum for a comedic actor when he was paid $20 million dollars to star in a movie. Today Jim continues to dare to dream big dreams and constantly reinvents himself as an actor by going outside of his comfort zone and doing new things. He too consistently applies the one big thing again and again in his business very successfully.

Was it by chance or luck that Jim was able to accomplish his big dream—or the fact that he carried his dream around with him every day to keep him focused and going in the direction of his daring big goal?

You become what you think about most of the time. Of course, while searching for any treasure, it helps to have a road map and the keys to secret doors. We begin right now with Secret No.1.

Okay, it's not really a secret; you may just not know it yet.

Identify your big daring dream.

Dream it.

Then do it.

What Business School Did Not Teach You

Stop hiding out and playing small. It's your turn to shine!

"You gain strength, courage, and confidence by every experience in which you really start to look fear in the face. You must do the thing which you think you cannot do." ~ *Eleanor Roosevelt*

I am often asked, "What is the real secret of success?" And in my opinion are there many shortcuts to achieving success in business. The kinds of things you need to know, but the ones they don't teach in business school. The greatest secret to being highly successful in business, whether you are a realtor, mortgage broker, or a business owner, is that there are no secrets.

You have to follow your heart and do what you know is right for you. There are as many ways to define success as there are people in business and what works for one person is not guaranteed to work for another.

There are two important things that can guarantee success in business, and keep in mind that most people ignore this advice. The first is to "dream big daring dreams," and the other is to "do what you love." Not exactly the type of advice you hear in traditional business schools, is it? Yet it's effective, challenging, and highly practical.

Too many times I meet people who are bored to tears, miserable, dissatisfied, frustrated, or angry that the business they have isn't the way that they want it to be. Yet they stick it out year after year.

Why?

Is it fear of failure? Lack of energy? Lack of get-up-and-go?

Surely it can't be because they are afraid of potential joy, contentment, personal satisfaction and a sense of fulfillment.

Changing direction isn't the same thing as giving up or failure; rather, it is an acknowledgment that what you've been doing up to now isn't giving you what you want or need in business. Just because you begin your business one way doesn't mean you can't change and do something else when you discover what your true passion is.

Eva, a client of mine, worked her butt off to get known and recognized in her field. She was in the right business, but had the wrong approach to increasing her influence, impact, and income. No matter what she did, or how much marketing she did, she was unable to fill her practice. During our sessions I found out that she has a love for health so she decided to open a store that sold everything to do with being healthy—vitamins, energy bars, workout videos, massages, consulting sessions, you name it.

What was missing was being able to be successful at something that she truly loved. These limiting fears were hidden away in her unconscious yet were costing her enormous amount of freedom and joy in her business. We worked through her fears of charging what she was worth, asking for the money, doing sales presentations, and being perfect just to name a few. Once that happened things started to take off. Because she stopped hiding out and decided to play full out in her business, and was absolutely passionate about what she was doing, customers —and there are thousands of people out there who also love living a healthy lifestyle—came to her spa and salon, making it a remarkable success. On our last call, she told me she now had plans to open two more salons and it's easy to see that she loves every minute of her new way of being in business.

What exactly did she do to improve her situation?

What was the smart "think big" change that she made?

She wasn't feeling great about her business. She told me that she used to have such a passion for business, yet now, she was feeling disappointed, irritated with her clients, and burdened by a business that she had owned for so many years.

Her voice was listless, distant, even bordering miserable. She explained to me that what she really wanted (what was on the top of her list) was a closer, connected relationship with her clients, but because she was so busy growing her business she was unable to do that the way she used to. Her relationship with her clients had begun drifting apart when her clients were starting to see some successes, she didn't know how to connect with them again. This was causing her tremendous anxiety and sadness.

If you didn't delve a bit deeper to find out that she was really committed to change all of this, you might have thought that she had given up on her business to some extent just by the sound of her voice.

So, we started our work together to shift her mindset and weave a tapestry of healing throughout her business and relationships…a tapestry that would help her to overcome her constant complaining and finding fault with others to embracing compassion, communication, and success.

Some in the business world think success only has to do with money. Yet, you can have all the money in the world and still be unhappy within your business relationships because of some underlying issues around your mindset that you have yet to transform.

And this was Eva.

What some sales professionals don't realize about shifting your mindset is that first you must be allowing and committed in seeing a shift in your mindset. Then, for a true shift in mindset to occur, you must allow empathy to come flooding into your mind and your business.

So, what does a complete mindset shift look like?

After working together for a few weeks, Eva got on the phone with me for our session together. You should have heard her voice! I heard a completely different voice on the other end. Com-plete-ly.

She was energetic, excited, spilling over with good news.

She "got it" and had a big revelation from our "mind shifting" work together.

The revelation was that she needed transforming in all of the relationships in her business, not just with her clients.

She was writing love notes to her whole team. She was excited. She was feeling 'great' and laughing. She told me that she was going for her one big thing, her daring big dream.

Even her life partner told her that her voice had changed and that she was smiling more.

What I know from this work is that shifting your mindset is a crucial first step to success in your business and will unlock doors that you can't even conceive of from where you stand right now. And the money will follow.

Why?

Because you have subconscious limiting beliefs left over from your past or the way you were parented. When you're able to release these limiting beliefs and integrate new subconscious beliefs that completely support who you are, then you're really in for some awesome changes in your business.

So, what's a limiting belief?

A limiting belief is some belief that you're telling yourself over and over again. For many of us, we are not even sharing what this belief actually is because we feel ashamed, wrong, bad, or a lot of the times, you don't even know that it's there! It's happening on a subconscious level and can completely sabotage your business success of increasing your influence, impact and income!

Some examples of limiting beliefs are:

"I'm all alone in my business."

"I have to do this by myself."

"I'm not worthy."

"I'm not good enough."

"Nobody listens to me."

"I don't matter."

So, how can you shift your mindset right now?

Here are three tips for you to begin shifting your mindset right now:

Tip #1: Consciously Choose Your Media

> Shift what you listen to, externally and internally. Everything is frequency. Success means that you need to begin to tap into the frequency that you desire. Stop watching media that doesn't support your vision. Really. Write down and listen to your new beliefs…what will truly serve you and your business?

Tip #2: Cultivate Self-Empathy

> Empathy really means to get into another person's shoes.

> See business from another's perspective. When you can have empathy for yourself and allow yourself to have whatever emotions arise in any given moment without judgment or making them mean anything about you, then you allow yourself the space for change.

> Self-empathy sounds like "It's all ok. Whatever emotion is coming up for me, I'm going to honour it. Give it space. It will pass when I don't resist it. This emotion is necessary for my transformation and highest good."

Tip #3: Surround Yourself With Supportive People

> You may have heard the saying "You're only as good as the company you keep." Well, I have a new one for you: "You're only as successful as the mindset of the company you keep."

Mindset is everything. If you're surrounding yourself with people who are negative, judgmental, gossiping, or critical, then you may find yourself feeling dragged down. You want to surround yourself with positive people, people who are on your side, people with whom you feel safe sharing your dreams and passions, people who will lift you up and encourage the best in you.

Notice how you feel when you're around somebody.

Are you feeling happy and encouraged? Or judged and withdrawn?

Tip #4: The formula for success is far from being a secret, far from being unreachable.

It's about working through your fears and limits, coming out of hiding, doing something that you love to do, and then making it the focus of your business. It doesn't matter who you are, or what you do, go out and do something you love. Feel the pleasure of waking up in the morning and realizing that at last you're being honest with yourself. Face your fears and limited thinking, you're no longer struggling to have success, instead you've started to work like you mean it, you're having it your own way, and shining.

You'll be supported. You'll often find that when you stop playing small in your business you hear, "Good on you," and things like, "I wish I had the guts to do what you're doing." You will grin from ear to ear and know that the work you did to remove those old, tired limits and fears was well worth it. You'll hold your head a little higher. And while the immediate future may be tremendously uncertain, you will walk into it knowing that it's your future to make and that you're doing what you want to do. You simply followed your heart, and it's your time to shine.

We're taught from a young age to avoid errors and failure at all costs, yet as any successful creator or sales professional will prove, breakthroughs don't happen without them, as I have mentioned again and again throughout this book.

So we have to be willing (and able) to think outside of the box.

Instead of trying to build elaborate plans or perfect ideas, we need to make small, reasonable bets in order to learn quickly, build momentum and networks, and expand our abilities and resources in order to discover unique ideas and opportunities.

Consider how Twitter came about. It didn't happen overnight. Founder Jack Dorsey had been, in his words, "obsessed" by how people moved, interacted, and communicated since the early 1990s. So, he learned basic computer programming, created maps with dots on them, and used information from Manhattan dispatch systems to track the movement of bike messengers, taxis, police, firefighters, and couriers. It was a start of bigger things to come.

Dorsey then transferred to New York University and got a job as a programmer with the largest dispatch company in the world. He learned a lot in the role and eventually focused on the short format messages that people sent to large dispatch boards. "This became the basis for all of my work going forward," he recalled.

After moving to San Francisco in 2000, Dorsey continued to tinker with short messaging ideas. He started a company that dispatched emergency and taxi services from the web, but soon realized how little he knew about start-ups.

Coming at the end of the dot com era, the timing was bad, too. "The company was more or less a failure," he admitted.

Yet he would learn from it.

Dorsey continued to use instant messaging and LiveJournal (the early blogging platform) to post updates on what he was doing – simple things like, "I'm on the phone" or "I'm listening to the Black Eyed Peas." Once again, these were small, achievable steps toward Jack's larger interests, goals, and dreams.

Then one night, Dorsey couldn't sleep and sketched out an idea on a white board. The idea was to exchange short "status update" emails with friends using his RIM 850, a predecessor to the BlackBerry. The device had four lines of text good for short format messaging. Unfortunately, his friends didn't have RIM 850s.

So that experiment didn't go anywhere either, but Dorsey got little bit smarter, a little bit better, and a little bit closer to a big idea, the big dream, the big goal.

Around that time, Dorsey sketched out what would become the basis for Twitter several years later. On top it read "STATUS," followed by a short fill-in the blank where he wrote "Reading." But, lacking resources, Dorsey had to get a real job while continuing to tinker on the side.

Dorsey was eventually hired as an engineer at Odeo, a podcasting company where people weren't in love with podcasting. The company was, in fact, going nowhere, so founder Evan Williams asked employees for new ideas.

One night in 2006, Dorsey's colleague sent him the first text message he ever received. "I had no idea what this thing was," he remembered. But as Dorsey and his colleagues talked more about text messaging, he realized the short message format could be the missing link.

Williams gave him and another programmer 2 weeks to build the idea. After the model was a definite success internally at Odeo, Williams upped the ante for a six-month project, and then launched a full-scale version publically in July 2006. Twitter would consume more and more resources until Williams spun it off as a separate company in 2007.

Of course Dorsey's approach was brilliant. He focused like a laser on short messaging and made hundreds (if not thousands) of small, affordable bets in that area, most of which failed. But with each step he got slightly smarter, better, and closer, until he ultimately achieved a remarkable feat.

It's an approach that the best self-employed professionals and creators have learned to do well, but anyone can do it. Jack began when he was a programmer.

It began with a little bet that turned into a big goal, a big dream, and a big result.

What will yours be?

Negative People Are Rarely, If Ever, Content, and What to Do About It

Keep in mind: negative people are rarely, if ever, content.

"You are the average of the five people you spend the most time with." ~ *Jim Rohn*

In the many years that I have been a business and real estate trainer, mentoring and coaching clients around the world, a consistent theme in my programs, products, and services is that in business, absolutely everything counts. From the day we start our business until the day we leave the business, we are shaped by our surroundings—our business environment, our schooling, what we read, listen to, and watch, the friends and colleagues we associate with, our home environment, our life partners, the neighbors around us, and the communities we belong to. As a result, we become the quality of everything we see and do and it contributes to the evolving beings that we are in our business.

In addition to the idea that everything counts, I also talk about action and reaction and about manifesting what you put out into the world.

For every cause there is at least one effect. Its simple wisdom: everything counts and it is up to us to determine how much our business will count for. If we wish, we can go passively through business letting the influences of the world take over our minds and actions. We can also, if we choose, be completely unaware that we're part of anything at all. You've met sales professionals like this. You can talk to them about all kinds of frivolous things, but try to take the conversations to a deeper level and you hit a dead end.

I find that business owners who hit dead ends like this are very draining on the rest of us.

I lead a real estate mastermind group (a team that I mentor and coach) and once, for three weeks, I had people emailing me and asking me to not put them with one of the members in our brainstorming sessions. Out of 7 people, 4 had told me Negative Nellie (not her real name, of course) was too negative to mastermind and brainstorm with while on our calls.

So now I had a dilemma, what was I going to do? Talk to her about her attitude? Ask her to stop coming to the calls, even though she is a team member? Literally, every week the other people she masterminded with would approach me and ask me to NEVER put her with them again. This left me in a leadership dilemma as to how to turn this around without alienating her and I knew the group was watching to see how I would handle it.

So I partnered up with her personally for the next two weeks and observed her communication style. Negative Nellie is what I call a "socialized negative"-- she gets her attention and fulfillment by focusing on and sharing with you the negatives of her day and business. To her, she is connecting with you, while to others she was repelling them. I knew that if I talked to her about it she wouldn't be able to even "see" what I was saying as she saw what she did as "socializing," not as being negative.

When you run into someone like this, here are some tips on how to turn the negative person around so they stop draining you:

Ask only questions that can be answered positively.

Avoid any yes or no questions as opening conversation questions. Since the person's brain is conditioned to go negative they will want to answer those questions from the depressing side or point of view.

When they go negative, don't try to "solve" what they put out there. This only feeds the cycle and gets them to bring up more negative points.

If they carry on about something, ask them, "What are you expecting of me? Do you want to solve this?" If they say "Yes", then you immediately move them to focusing on how they will solve it. Remember to make them solve it, not you! If they say "No", then you simply say, "Okay since you don't want to solve it, it is best if we just let it go. So let's focus on..." and redirect the conversation.

In a team meeting or a mastermind session, if you have a negative person, make them play the "devil's advocate" and look at things from the opposite perspective. Give them time to do this, as, for them, it will be like pulling teeth.

People who are "socialized" negative just really want to connect and talk, but how they do it drives everyone crazy. They won't see that until they start getting more attention from people as they frame things into the positive.

If you have a negative person on your real estate or sales professional team or in your mastermind group, take this week to try to actively change the way you interact with them and see if you can move them toward more positive outcomes like I did in my group.

If only they would realize that taking other directions in business can offer such wonderfully fulfilling rewards. The catch is that it's a choice that each person needs to make for him or herself.

To determine whether their choices are taking them in the right direction, I often suggest to my clients and readers that they do a features and benefits assessments of themselves. This involves looking at the various areas of your mindset and business and applying a rating—on a scale of 1 to 10—of how well you are doing.

For instance, if you get along well with your clients and colleagues, give yourself an 8 in that area. However, if you get along exceptionally well with others, give yourself a 10.

What about follow-through? Do you follow up with tasks and responsibilities in a timely and effective manner in your business?

If so, you'll want to rate yourself at the high end of the scale.

In this manner, my clients and I continue going through a list of attributes that we all believe are essential to being a well-rounded realtor or broker and that would most likely contribute to success in business.

When we do this assessment, what we learn along the way—if we're honest, and why wouldn't we be?—is that all of us find some areas where we want to improve. And more often than not, it is because we have let the little things slip, things such as maintaining a growth mindset, charging what we are worth and being able to ask for it, getting enough exercise and rest, overcoming our negative thinking and fears, participating in community activities and giving back, and so on.

If we don't do this type of inventory from time to time and make adjustments to our behavior, we will soon discover that the accumulation of the little things will begin to affect our ability to increase our influence, impact and income in our business in a negative way—causing us to drift away from our dreams and goals, get less clients than we used to, be less able to participate in growing our business with fresh, new ideas, or find that we are disconnected from our community and our ability to give back.

It's a dreadful thought; we begin to remind ourselves of those self-absorbed individuals that we say we can't stand.

How can we keep this from taking place?

Business is complicated at times, even difficult. We need guiding principles to keep us headed in the directions we want to go in to increase our influence, impact and income. When we don't have these, it's easy to get pulled down by even the smallest of details.

In all my years of doing business, I have learned that everything operates much better in my world when I'm working to a plan and I can line up all of the various areas of my business according to the goals and ideals that I have set out for myself. Having a balanced plan and doing a recurring personal assessment inventory are just two guiding principles that help me to stay on track in my business. As a bonus, this allows you to relax more, laugh more, and play more.

They can help you too. Start by doing a personal assessment inventory now to establish where you're at in different areas of your mindset and business. Based on your assessment, you can see which areas need work and plan how you will make changes to improve your overall score. If you don't by now have both short-and longer-term goals written down, it's a great time to do that as well.

After a few months, do another assessment to measure your growth and evolution. If you set a short-term goal, have you reached it? If you said that you would make some changes in your negative mindset, what have you done to move in that direction? If you're not happy with your current level of client attraction and lead generation activity, what changes have you made in your mindset and marketing?

This exercise works best if you keep a record of your growth and make a commitment to be really honest. Remember, you don't have to answer to anyone but yourself, but who could be better at asking the right questions?

The quality of everything we see and do plays a part in the person we are becoming. If you want to become a content, confident business owner, leave the negativity at the door.

Go From Being a Hostage in Your Business to Being Indispensable

Don't let your business to be taken prisoner by someone else's ego, insecurity and greed!

"The worst disease which can afflict business executives in their work is not, as popularly supposed, alcoholism; it's egotism." ~ Harold Geneen

Do you ever feel like you're a like a chess piece in someone else's game; a powerless player that is frequently used, abused and manipulated for the gain and self interest of others in business? Or do you come across self interest that's often thinly disguised as some kind of action, decision or "plan" that's somehow not in your best interest? Isn't it incredible how some self-called guru's know what's best for their business and yours? If only you and I had the ability to think and choose for ourselves; things could be so different. Have you ever felt like your business (or part of your business) has been taken prisoner by someone else's ego, insecurity, or greed?

Welcome to a very large club in the business world.

Gurus, Experts and Others

Perhaps you feel like you're trapped in some kind of on-going poker game where you're never dealt any good cards in your business. As a result you feel like you have no real influence, impact or leverage… just the rare bluff. The truth is, knowingly or not, many of us have given away our personal power (or part thereof) and allowed situations, circumstances and other people to dictate, direct and control our reality. Some of us have let so-called gurus and experts tell us what we can do and what we can't do in our business growth.

Being humble, generous and occasionally selfless sales professional is to be admired and respected, but being a sales professional who has essentially handed over the wheel of their business is heartbreaking, sad, and ultimately fatal. An agent or broker who has given away their personal power is an agent or broker who has given away control, hope and happiness. They have also given away their ability to dare to dream big.

It's nice to be nice but it's foolish to be a walked all over.

Some in business confuse feelings with reality. Not "feeling" powerful doesn't necessarily compare to not "being" powerful; unless we make it that. For the most part, feelings (read, fear) merely get in the way of our potential, personal power, growth, daring to dream big, and success. As a rule, our emotions and thoughts are in no way an indicator of our potential or the incredible future we might create and results we might produce if we should choose to use our power rather than give it away — as we have done in the past. Just because you don't "feel" powerful or consider yourself to be powerful doesn't mean that you're not or you can't be; it simply means you're denying your potential and buying into a fearful, limiting mindset. A feeling is only a feeling and a thought is only a thought until you make them a reality; good or bad.

Just to clarify and to point out how important this piece is:

We give away our power – the gurus, experts and others can't take it without our permission;

We allow people and things to have an unhealthy level of control and influence, becoming hostages in our own businesses.

Getting angry, cynical and/or resentful at others will fix nothing;

Positive growth and change starts with awareness, understanding and acknowledgement; and

The situation will change when you change – and you can change any time you chose. When you improve the relationship with yourself, you can start to become more indispensable to others.

Even as you read this right now, some of you might be rationalizing your less-than-desirable existence and situation in your business to make yourselves feel better and to evade confronting the things you know you should deal with. When you deal with them, your world will change.

You have the ability, you have the understanding and you have the reasons – now find the courage and confidence.

Time to Rock the Boat

So far I have mentioned the inclination that some of us have to allow situations, circumstances, events, and even experts, gurus and others to control our business; in essence, giving away our power in an attempt to be accepted, valued, appreciated, and loved. By trying to "not rock the boat" it seems that some of us have lost our identity and sense of self.

The good news is that we can take back control of our business and still be that thoughtful, generous and caring realtor – who also happens to be strong, confident, assertive, productive, indispensable, daring to dream big, successful, and powerful.

And no, we don't need to compromise our beliefs, goals, and character or core values to do so. In fact, taking back our power can be the most critical step towards fulfilling our true purpose, in alignment with our core values, integrity, and joy.

While the following strategies are very effective, they are not always comfortable or easy to implement, so it's a good thing that you and I are all about doing what works – not what's easy!

Get real, stop looking for easy and start "doing" effective.

All too often our desire to live a comfy, effortless, easy, and safe existence is the very thing that destroys our potential, our productivity, our ability to develop, and ultimately, our ability to dare to dream really big. It is no coincidence that we have both a widespread dislike to anything that makes us uncomfortable and so do a large number of brokers and agents who often feel frustrated, unfulfilled, lost and miserable. Ironically, it is our aversion to working against resistance that stops us from growing, learning, evolving and adapting. Sometimes we believe it's simply easier to just "put up and shut up", than to compromise and to bite our tongue.

While this is understandable every once in a while, over the long term this kind of behavior and thinking will set us up for unhealthy business relationships, stagnation, disconnection, irritation, desperation, and misery. In order to take back your power you will need to be courageous, you will need to be prepared to get uncomfortable, and you will need to do things that may make other people unhappy.

For instance, I've heard many stories from clients about bosses raging in meetings or getting in their employees' faces and berating them for mistakes or even shaming employees in front of others. This kind of outrageous behavior is abusive. If this is happening in your place of work, never silently take it. Your silence will lead to resentment and will chip away at your sense of self-worth.

If your boss is being disrespectful or abusive, address the behavior directly and in the moment. If there are a lot of people around and you don't feel comfortable doing it with an audience, request that your boss speak with you immediately following the incident. For example; a client of mine said to her boss, "Mr. Jones, I'd like to speak with you about the meeting today. Can we please schedule 15 minutes to do that?"

Once you are sitting down with your boss, own your mistake. If you were wrong, state the behavior you didn't like and ask for what you want now and/or in the future.

Be sure to be clear, to the point and specific about what you want. My client said: "Mr. Jones, I apologize for not proofreading the document I handed you. I will not make that same mistake again. I want you to know, however, that the way you gave me that feedback did not feel okay for me. I do not like to be yelled at anywhere in my life—work included. I would like for you to discuss things with me in private and to do so in a respectful tone. Are you willing to do this?"

After you have spoken, the ball is in your boss's court. Pay attention to how they respond. If they become angry, then it's likely that you do not have a "workable" situation. If they stay calm, hear you out and apologize, then there's hope. Either way, their reaction is data for you. If they get angrier, I would try to set limits a couple more times to see if they're open to taking your feedback in. If you hit the same result every time, I would start planning my exit like my client did.

Come out of hiding and face your hidden fears: You can never take back your power until you confront the things that scare you.

"Show me the entrepreneur who fears nothing and I'll show you a fake."

If things only have the power and influence that we assign them, then fear is something we can control and use for our own personal development.

For the most part fear is a completely personal thing. It's not about the situation, circumstance or environment but rather US in it; how we react to, process, cope with, and interpret the events in our business. That's why we can see two people doing the exact same thing at the same time (growing their business for example); one is excited and having a great time, while the other is terrified and having the worst time ever. That's because it isn't about the growth; it's about the grower. Keep in mind that each grower (entrepreneur) creates his or her own reality. Of course there are healthy fears – not wanting to swim with a shark for example – but what we're talking about here are those destructive and unhealthy fears that have been known to make sales professionals prisoners of their own mind, for a lifetime.

The Italian sculptor Agostino d'Antonio worked diligently on a large piece of marble. Unable to produce his desired masterpiece, he lamented and gave into his fears, "I can do nothing with it." Other sculptors also worked this difficult piece of marble, but to no avail. Michelangelo discovered the stone and visualized the possibilities in it. His "I-can-make-it-happen" attitude worked through any fears and resulted in one of the world's masterpieces - David.

When nice isn't really about being nice.

Seek to be strong rather than nice. Too many nice realtors go broke because all they have is a bunch of "nice-ness" and zero personal power.

34

Sometimes nice-ness is actually a euphemism for weakness and far too often our need to be seen as the "nice business person" is what bankrupts us. Trying to keep everyone in your business happy is an exercise in futility, frustration, and exhaustion. It's also foolishness. In short, it won't happen. It's not your job to "make" people happy; it's your job to be the best version of you. And not the "you" that people want you to be, but rather your authentic self. Your authentic self has clarity, certainty, contentment, and calm about whom and what you are in business. And no, being you does not mean being selfish; it's about self care.

Stop playing the victim card.

Business isn't fair. The majority of people around you don't care about you or your issues. Stuff happens. Bad things happen to good sales people. Lots of entrepreneurs are selfish, boastful and nasty. There are more than enough who are not. Now, stop seeking pity, attention and sympathy and get on with it. Stop having the same futile discussions about the same issues and playing the victim card, and stop waiting to be "saved" in your business. Stop giving away your power. You don't need universal approval, acceptance or endorsement, or another guru or expert; you need a different mindset.

Win real respect through your inspired actions.

Talk less in your business, think more and do more. What you do will tell the rest of us far more about whom you are than any words that might come out of your mouth. Talk is cheap and often meaningless. Most big talkers are just that, and nothing more. Get moving towards something that is daring, inspiring, big, and bold, and something that excites you.

Henry Ford once hired an efficiency expert to go through his plant. He said, "Find the non-productive people. Tell me who they are, and I will fire them!"

The expert made the rounds with his clipboard in hand and finally returned to Henry Ford's office with his report. "I've found a problem with one of your administrators," he said. "Every time I walked by, he was sitting with his feet propped up on the desk. The man never does a thing. I definitely think you should consider getting rid of him!" When Henry Ford learned the name of the man the expert was referring to, Ford shook his head and said, "I can't fire him. I pay that man to do nothing but think - and that's what he's doing."

Keep re-inventing yourself and move closer to becoming the best version of yourself.

Being stagnant in your business growth and inflexible in a world full of opportunities is a sure-fire way to become redundant, unnecessary, limited, and powerless. While your core values, beliefs, and standards might stay constant, it is important that you continue to adapt, learn, grow, and develop with your ever-changing business growth.

Nicolo Paganini was a well-known and gifted nineteenth century violinist. He was also well known as a great showman with a quick sense of humor. His most memorable concert was in Italy with a full orchestra. He was performing before a packed house and his technique was incredible, his tone was fantastic, and his audience dearly loved him. In other words, he was running a very successful business that he loved. Toward the end of his concert one night, Paganini was astounding his audience with an unbelievable composition when suddenly one string on his violin snapped and hung limply from his instrument. Paganini frowned briefly, shook his head, and continued to play, improvising beautifully.

Then, to everyone's surprise, a second string broke, and shortly thereafter, a third. Almost like a slapstick comedy, Paganini stood there with three strings dangling from his Stradivarius. But instead of leaving the stage, Paganini stood his ground, reinvented himself in that moment, learned to hang in there, maintained his strong work ethic, and calmly completed the difficult number on the one remaining string. We can reinvent ourselves in a moment or gradually over a lifetime. You get to decide.

Value yourself and increase your value.

Stop treating others in business and around you as though they are of greater worth than you. Nobody is more important than anyone else.

Furthermore, nobody is more important than you. No one. This is not about having a massive ego or being self-righteous; it's about stopping all the self-sabotage. It's about not rationalizing mediocrity and failure any more. It's about changing your standards and your thinking. It's about not letting your poor self-esteem get in the way of your potential, possibilities and daring to dream really big dreams. It's about not letting your past become your future. You are worthy, you are talented, you are good enough and you are powerful. More than you may be aware of.

Boldly protect your positioning and branding.

Never associate with people, experts, gurus, businesses, situations, programs, products or services that will damage or destroy your reputation. In the business world you're positioning and brand is your power. It's your money in the bank. The stronger you're positioning and brand, the more power you have in business. Leads, potential business associates, and current customers will all "buy what you're selling" based mostly on their perception of you; your product, your service, your programs, your ability, your skill, your integrity, and your value to them.

Business Beauty School: Improve the Relationship with Yourself!

You are beautiful inside out, when you develop a strong relationship with yourself!

"The thing always happens that you really believe in; and the belief in a thing makes it happen." ~ *Frank Lloyd Wright*

I have learned a lot about what makes sales professionals feel attractive, and be attractive on the inside as they wake up from auto-pilot (working and responding in a robotic way) and become the best version of them. And by that I don't mean which over-the-counter remedy works best or how to get just the right nip or tuck that leads to looking like the latest model on a magazine cover. What I mean is what really works, what really counts, what really matters and that is what is going on inside of you, your mindset and current thinking for those of you who want to feel and look great. This is because the strength and clarity of your inner mindset, relationship with yourself, and best kind of thinking and mindset for growth and success is critical at any stage of your business.

Having worked with brokers and agents who have a growth mindset and that big, flexible thinking that helps create outer beauty—as a business mentor, mindset and marketing coach, and trainer—I discovered trade secrets from those whose businesses were all about becoming the best version of themselves and to be the best they can. (Yes, our objective was to make it to the top of our chosen careers and dare to have big dreams!) As a business owner for more than 20 years, I came to have a different daring big dream, vision and goal: to help other business owners understand them so they can feel, look and position themselves at their best and improve their inner game, inner relationship, and growth mindset. My career led me to see patterns in the thousands of business owners that I have worked with and find the answers to, "What really makes business owners feel attractive in their thinking from the inside out in their businesses?" I mentored thousands of business owners—current and former sales professionals, corporate execs, mortgage brokers, realtors, and people from all walks of life. Your responses revealed a number of surprising similarities and are summarized here. I call it Business Beauty School. These are habits that work from the inside out to create inner beauty from your thinking in the way that reflects that thinking and results to your outside world.

Show Strong Confidence from the Inside

The most frequent comment I have heard from sales professionals is that outer beauty is created by having strong inner confidence and the best kind of thinking and mindset for growth and success. The comment resonated with something that my first business mentor told me the first day I worked with her. She said, "The chance of building a 6 figure meaningful business for us rises the minute you take on an air of strong inner confidence, the best mindset and thinking no matter how long you have been in business." I learned pretty quickly that success isn't about being the smartest—everyone is.

Nor is it about being perfect—no one is. It is about how you carry yourself.

This is because of the strong inner confidence you create, having a solid relationship with yourself, having the best kind of thinking and mindset for growth and success, and then how self-assured you position yourself and appear to the outside world. So is it for all who have been in business for any length of time. Holding your head up high, stepping into the spotlight with poise and strong inner self-confidence, and having a rock solid relationship with yourself is probably the number one quality that business owners say leads to feeling and having a strong sense of inner beauty. You gain this confidence by having best kind of thinking and mindset for growth and success and passion no matter how long you have been in business.

Focus on What You Do Have, Not on What You Don't!

The sum is not always greater than the whole of its parts. Sounds counterintuitive, but when it comes to feeling beautiful on the inside, having a rock solid great relationship with yourself, having the best kind of thinking and mindset for growth and success, and daring your big dreams it's important to keep this in mind. Agents and brokers who focus on characteristics, qualities, benefits and features they like (rather than those they don't) and use them to serve their self-image, influence, impact, positioning, and authority in their chosen fields are more likely to say you feel attractive on the inside and out. You develop that strong relationship with yourself, best kind of thinking and mindset for growth and success and can work through anything that comes your way.

Some of you are branded for your great marketing or keen sense of trends in business, for instance. You use these skills as positioning to get buyers, sellers, customers and sales. Sometimes only you or what you know is marketable in your business. How can standing out and succeeding on your own terms make everything else about you look and feel more attractive from the inside out? By having a strong relationship with you and having the best kind of thinking and mindset for growth and success.

Reinvent You

Flexibility is absolutely essential. Instead of holding onto old definitions of inner beauty, such as worrying about what others think of you, or feeling anxious about change as you are fulfilling your big dreams, sales professionals who find fun in reinventing their positioning, social influence, branding, and look are able to feel attractive from the inside. This is because they have that solid relationship with themselves as they grow their businesses through the years. Holding on and holding back is limiting and causes individuals to get left behind in business. Moving forward and letting go of old fears, limits, blocks, and barriers help you appear relaxed and that is what will show up when people view you in your business. Remember, letting go of your former negative self-image, your limited and fixed mindset, your old brand, social influence or positioning doesn't mean losing business. It's like learning to enjoy writing when you may have sourced it out in the past or taking a copy-writing course in place of a standard writing course.

Having a flexible attitude and developing a strong inner relationship with you is moving towards becoming the best version of yourself and creating stronger inner beauty. This leads you to the ability to adjust your positioning, marketing, social influence, and branding sense and is key to enjoying your business at any length of time that you have been in business.

Relevance and Being Meaningful

As you build your business and your empires, you may leave behind some passion and lose sight of your purpose, vision, and your daring dreams. Because of the better relationship that you have with yourself, you never have to leave behind your abilities to connect to others in a relevant and meaningful way. Many agents and brokers who I have worked with or spoken to said that relevance and being meaningful was equated with feeling and looking attractive because they were so connected to themselves—from being a newbie to middle years of being in business and beyond.

During the course of building a business for the long haul, agents and brokers are often told to "do it like everyone else does it." However, some of the old school thinking in business can have sales look cold and dull no matter how connected a person may be on the inside to their own vision and mission. Just doing it like everyone else may work for a while for some, and the gods or universe above may bless them, but they still have to look into the mirror every morning.

People who report feeling attractive as they grow their businesses for the long haul say you never forget your capacity to be relevant and meaningful and want to hold onto it now in your business and beyond.

Leave Competition Out of Creating Real Inner Beauty and Strength

It's important to remember that inner beauty is about creating a strong relationship with yourself and becoming the best version of you for however length of time you are in business rather than competing with others. Successful sales professionals whose careers last the longest learn that lesson early on. From the day you start working, there is always going to be another younger, smarter, more confident person ready to take your place. So you manage best by creating the strong invincible relationship with yourself, looking forward, being future focused, and daring to dream big, rather than looking sideways or backward. You can get caught up comparing yourselves to younger, smarter, confident agents. Those who say they feel attractive because of the strong relationship with themselves as they grow your businesses are interested in looking and feeling robust and vital.

This is not because they want to be the newbie again in business as they once were, but because inner confidence causes one to care about how they look and feel on the outside. You don't focus on having the perfect marketing plan, the magic bullet to success, short-term gain, or short-term vision or your big dreams. You feel like a winner, not because you come in first in your business as highly successful, but because you get out of a race you know you can't win. You can then channel your energy into achieving your personal best and creating a strong relationship with yourself from the inside out, the best kind of thinking and mindset for growth and success, and becoming the best version of you as you grow and age in your business experiences.

Mindset: Why Some Realtors and Sales Professionals Think Small and Play Small and What to Do About It

"Success consists of going from failure to failure without loss of enthusiasm." ~ Winston Churchill

Mindset shapes our mental world, influences our outlook, determines how big or small our goals and dreams, and in due course sets us on a path of growth and fulfillment, or one of stagnation. Every kind of business imaginable is filled with successful people who know they are smart, and have had amazing results and achievements. Still, some stagnate, while others dare to dream big dreams and thrive while continuing to become the best version of them and really shine.

The mindset we build and grow over the years, that was in the beginning influenced by our caretakers, teachers and bosses, can apply a powerful grip on our approach toward continuous learning and achieving. In fact, it's the key to success and fulfillment, explaining why high IQ's fail to effectively forecasts success.

More importantly, mindset may be an important clue as to why some sales professionals fall short of their dreams and goals and why some are more prone than others to the mindset of what is called "dis-ease."

Our mindset is the view of the whole world, not just our business and the world that we live in with our family. Our mindset determines whether we will have a positive or negative outlook on the world. It literally shapes our dreams and goals and our outlook and approach towards our business, clients, and vendors. And of course, it will predict whether we become the best version of ourselves and fulfill our fullest potential and all of our big daring dreams and goals.

Two Kinds of Mindsets in Business

Sales professionals and realtors have two chief kinds of mindsets. You either have a closed or fixed kind of mindset or an open, or growth kind of mindset in business.

The closed mindset is deep-rooted in the belief that natural talents and abilities determine success and whether or not you will fulfill your dreams and goals.

The open mindset is open to growth, change, learning, and fully believing that you can always do better, and be better than where you are now, outshine your past, and improve you future.

With a closed mindset, business owners believe success is based on their natural talents; so, they shouldn't have to work as hard. They think their abilities are set and can never be changed or improved. Either you have them or you don't.

You must prove yourself again and again, trying to look smart and talented no matter what the cost or sacrifice. This is the sure-fire path to stagnation.

Business owners with a closed mindset seek validations of their worth and want to be right, instead of showing an interest in feedback and readiness to make changes, amendments or adjustments.

With an open mindset, business owners believe they can always learn more, do more, be more, and improve. They are confident, yet humble enough to work harder to expand to become the best version of them, live their full potential and help more people.

If you have an open mindset, you know your talents can be developed and that great abilities are built over time. This is the real path to opportunity and success, as well as fulfilling your big dreams and goals.

YOUR MINDSET TEST

Which mindset do you have about your own intelligence?

• Your intelligence is something very fundamental that cannot change very much at all.

• You can learn new things, but you can't really change how intelligent you are, you are born the way that you are and that's it.

• No matter how intelligent you are, you can always improve and grow.

• You can substantially and significantly change how intelligent you are.

How did you do? Well, statements one and two reflect a fixed or closed mindset. Statements three and four indicate an open or growth mindset. Some of you can fall somewhere in the middle, but most are inclined to bend towards one direction more than the other.

You also have beliefs about your other abilities as well. Try substituting marketing talent, artistic talent, creative talent, a specific business talent, or skill for intelligence, and see where you are inclined to be.

The Drawback of Natural Talent

When you believe your natural abilities determine your success, you don't see a call to learn or work harder. Sales professionals with fixed or closed mindsets spend their energy promoting and defending what they consider their exceptional talents, instead of being fully open to learning something new and something different. They also refuse to come clean about their mistakes and correct their weaknesses, as they're obsessed with shielding their positions of status and point their energies to emphasizing their image of self-importance. They want to verify their worth to others, and they are inclined to rely on their previous accomplishments, standing, and status symbols.

If every bit of information and feedback about your beloved qualities signifies either good news or bad news, as it does for closed and fixed minded business owners, falsehoods predictably takes place. Some outcomes are overblown, while others are explained away to uphold one's image and highly coveted sense of self-importance.

Extraordinary sales people have a special knack for discovering their own strengths and weaknesses. They have open minds and are willing to take in feedback about their own weaknesses so they can improve themselves and their business performance.

Individuals with a closed mindset, on the other hand, take in only the information that supports their view of themselves, and they're more concerned with appearing self-important and most importantly, right. As a result, they simply twist information so they'll look good no matter the cost.

A closed mind leads to "dis-ease," categorized by information that's filtered and twisted so only good news flows out and flows to the top. Their surrounding team repeatedly plays its part by nourishing the person's ego.

Business owners and the Big E-word

When did sales and big ego become one and the same? There is a huge belief that just as there are naturals in music and golf, there are also naturals in business. This has become known as the "talent mindset." This kind of professional is rewarded for their talents, and on the whole can do no wrong, and even if they do, they are hardly, if ever confronted or taken issue with, as their much beloved image would be threatened.

The problem is, those who use their status like peacocks are always looking for the next self-image boost. It's like taking a favorite drug; they just want more and more of it. They seldom think long- term business wellbeing for everyone involved. A good example of this would be Jeffrey Skilling and Kenneth Lay of the Enron disaster.

These men are prime examples of fixed and closed mindsets. They believed some business owners are naturally exceptional, had the necessity to prove, demonstrate, and show off their arrogance, and used their team players surrounding them to feed this need instead of creating team development and growth for all. In the end, as we all know, they sacrificed their business and their companies to get their fix.

The Open and Growth Mindset

This is the type of business owner who dares to dream big, and while dreaming big guides and grows a business and everyone in it to true and lasting greatness. Someone with a big ego is one who shouts from the rooftops how gifted and talented they are to anyone who will listen.

Someone with an open mindset, on the other hand, is unassuming, continually asks questions, and has the knack to face up to the brutal answers. They look failures straight in the eye, including their own, while sustaining faith that they'll succeed no matter what.

These sales professionals have an open and growth mindset:

• They aren't continually trying to establish they're better and outshine others.

• They don't point out their position and always remind others who is at the top.

• They don't claim recognition for other people's contributions or help.

• They don't undermine and undercut others to feel more powerful and in control.

Instead these kinds of sales professionals:

Are always improving and growing.

Surround them with the most talented, intelligent and competent people they can find.

Look directly at their own mistakes and weaknesses and work through them.

Recognize the skills that they and their businesses will need in the future, and implement what needs to happen to make that a reality.

These qualities allow sales professionals to move forward with confidence, courage, and cojones; built on facts, not on fantasies about their own gifts and genius.

Open mindset individuals aren't afraid of discussion, examination, debates, or questioning. They dig deep to uncover realities and weaknesses.

Recovering From a Closed Mindset

The influence and power some brokers and agents have allows them to generate a world that caters to their need for validation. It protects them from bad news and it encourages them to believe in their fantasies that they have created around their business success, despite any warning signs or messages to the contrary.

There is however, a cure for "dis-ease" In business. Everyone can change their mindset. It involves having a mindful practice, watchfulness, and a willingness to be open to learning, growing and changing. Yet, it's not easy to let go of something that has felt like your "true self" for many years and has served as your continuous path to self-esteem. It's particularly tough to replace it with a mindset that involves you embracing issues that feel threatening: challenges, being daring, resistance, criticism, and setbacks.

Remember, people take on a closed mindset because it protects them from feeling vulnerable. But opening yourself up to growth allows you to experience the fulfillment of your real potential and fulfilling big and daring dreams. The resulting rewards of fulfilling those dreams and the path along the way will become self-reinforcing.

One essential key to successfully changing your mindset is to ask for guidance. It may be helpful to engage a coach or mentor to help guide you through the transformation so they can catch your blind spots.

Think of something you really need to do or want to learn. Is there a problem you're forced to deal with? Now, make a concrete, specific step-by-step plan.

For example: "tomorrow, I'll contact that expert coach that I follow on Facebook and ask them to help me through my self-imposed limits and beliefs. I'll set up some sessions, ask good questions, and receive feedback, without acting defensive. I won't make excuses. I'll take in information, be receptive and thank them for their input. I can decide what to do later, after I get more information or guidance."

Detailed and comprehensive plans that cover where, when, and how you're going to do something leads to high levels of follow-through and significantly increases your chances of success. Even if you have critical and negative thinking and feelings, you must carry through your growth-oriented plan.

Creating change can be tough, but it's always worth it, as you can see from the stories that I have shared in this book. An open mindset allows you to feel more vibrant, vital and valued, and it will increase your chances for success at your full potential and to fulfilling your big dreams.

How to Grow Your Mindset and Realize Your Big Dreams

Are you a sales professional with a closed mindset or an open mindset in your business? Ask yourself the following questions, which encourage an open and growth mindset. Be honest, the only person you will cheat is yourself if you aren't, but then of course, why wouldn't you be?

Answer these questions:

- Do you feel others are evaluating and then judging you, or they helping you to grow and develop?

- Are there ways you can be less defensive about your mistakes and slip-ups?

- Could you benefit more from the feedback and comments you get?

- Are there ways to generate more learning experiences for you?

- How do you act towards others in front of them and when they are not there?

- Where's your frequent focus? Is it on your influence and control, or your client's and team's long term well-being?

- Do you ever reaffirm your rank and position by humiliating or shaming others?

- Do you ever attempt to hold back high-performing team members because they intimidate you?

- Do you think about ways to help your team members develop and grow through mentoring and coaching?

- Do you think about how you can treat your team, and clients as collaborators, and promote and encourage teamwork?

- Do you try to create a culture of self-examination, open communications and teamwork in your business surroundings?

- How can you encourage alternative views, opinions, outlooks and constructive criticism?

Be an Example of Daring to Dream Big

Perhaps the best tip I have heard from those in real estate who are making a big difference in the world gracefully is to see you as a role model for the next generation.
You feel a responsibility to demonstrate that being attractive from the inside out, having a great relationship with yourself, and having the best kind of thinking and mindset for growth and success is not only a possibility, but that the meaning of inner beauty and developing that relationship with yourself can be broadened and deepened with the length of time that you are in business.

When you have an open mindset you don't panic as your business changes over the years, so your inner relationship and outer thinking appear calm, confident and relaxed. As a social influencer, you show the kind of poise and grace you want your clients, friends, and younger colleagues to emulate. You say you owe it to yourself and others to look forward optimistically to the years that lie ahead in your business so that you pass on that kind of confidence to others. Having inner strength, a strong relationship with yourself, and the best kind of thinking and mindset for growth, success, and beauty is reflected proudly on your face, in you mind, and in your business for all to see.

Why Working Through Your Blocks Helps You Succeed Faster and With Less Effort

You can't change what you don't face up to and own.

"Some people succeed because they are destined to, but most people succeed because they are determined to." ~ *Author Unknown*

I would encourage you to get really honest with yourself about your business and everybody in it. Be a straight shooter about what isn't working in your business. End all the excuses and start making changes that will improve your influence, impact and income.

Possibly, this part of the formula, more than any other, seems obvious. And to some extent, it is. If you're reluctant to face up to a belief, situation, problem, condition, behavior, or emotion—if you won't take ownership or your part in a situation—then you cannot and will not change it. If you refuse to face up to and own your own self-destructive behaviors, they will in fact grow momentum, become deeper rooted in the habitual patterns of your business, and grow more and more resistant to change.

Imagine your business and marketing coach asking you whether you've been having problems getting and keeping your ideal clients, and rather than come clean about it, you say, "Well no, not really." What's going to happen? The marketing coach isn't going address the problem and you'll keep getting the same poor results that you have been getting. She might change your tactics to something that doesn't work for your target market, but because you have lied to her, she may never deal with the real underlying problem. Because the marketing coach assumes that you are currently happy with your client attraction and lead generation results, she trusts you to identify your problems for her so she'll know where to focus her efforts.

You very likely believe that you can rely on yourself in a similar way. Just as the marketing coach depends on you to be brutally honest with her, you depend on yourself to be a straight shooter with yourself. If by denying the existence of a problem, you reap obvious benefits for evading a painful subject, and that makes you anything but a trustworthy source of information.

If you hope to have a winning business approach, you have to be honest about where your mindset and business are right now. The link between knowing exactly where you are in your business right now and where you want your business to be should be evident. Suppose you're out there, struggling with your business, wandering from idea to idea, and you call me on the phone and ask, "I'm so lost, how do I get unstuck?" My first question would be, "Well where are you now?"

Clearly, if you tell me that you are having trouble with your client attraction and lead generation, I'm going to give you directions and guidance very different from those I would give you if I learned you were struggling with client retention. The same holds true for the direction I might give to you for changing your mindset: if you stated for example, that your thinking was absolutely negative and fearful, I'd approach the situation differently than I would if you told me that your thinking was unlimited and full of possibilities.

If you told me that you are in a sticky situation of being unable to charge what you're worth and get it, and its draining you emotionally, and physically, I would go in a very different direction than I would if you told me that you were self-confident and on top of asking for and getting the money you deserve. Likewise, if you lie to yourself about any aspect of your thinking surrounding your business, you can distort the entire picture so much that an otherwise sound strategy will be compromised.

You can lie to yourself in two ways:

You can misrepresent the truth, or you can lie to yourself by leaving out certain things. Failing to tell yourself the truth is just as precarious as misrepresenting it. So you have to have the backbone and courage to ask yourself the tough questions, and to give yourself truthful answers.

Right now, you may be thinking: "Beverly, I don't even know what questions to ask to get to the truth, let alone the answers." That's all right; we will do this together, once you have some more tools you'll need in order to do it right. The point now is that you have to be willing to allow every belief, every situation, and every pattern in your business to be questioned, looked at, and challenged. When we talk about a truth, you have to be prepared to honestly assess your beliefs, positions, and patterns against that truth. You must drop all the defensiveness, lies, and denial. Denial, after all, is what destroys daring to dream really big dreams. It destroys hope. It destroys what might have been a real opportunity to overcome a problem had the solution just been followed sooner. Denial can, quite literally, destroy you if you let it.

I don't say that to be over the top; I say it because it's really true. In almost every kind of business and field, I've seen the heartbreaking effect of denial, and I'll bet that you have, too. It's time to deal with the denial in your own thinking and business. Let's begin by distinguishing that, in all business owners, there's a seldom-discussed self-protective defense system that we have.

It protects us from those things in our minds that, at some level, we cannot handle or which we do not want to face. It is almost like we have a "discerning memory" that takes effect.

It's active in your business every day. It can and does keep you from seeing things you just do not want to be true. In many situations, it may block you from picking up warning signs that, if you faced up to them, could trigger you to take essential and timely steps to help you manage the situation. Perhaps this defence system keeps you from being aware of the fact that your customers are less than pleased with your services. Maybe it blinds you to the worsening in your team's negative attitude towards you, allowing further distance and harm to take place. This defence can keep you from recognizing the warning signs of a serious gaping hole in your business systems that has you leaving money on the table, and, if detected and improved early, could be contained or made to become profitable. It can keep you from seeing the warning signs of any number of negative behaviors in your clients, such as showing up late for appointments, often paying late, or never doing what they say they will do.

Your blind spot may be the very things in your business that you most need to see. Denial and the defense underlie it, and touch your business in more ways that you could ever envision.

Problems rarely get better with time. You cannot change what you don't face up to and own. And what you do not face up to and own is going to get even worse until you do. Now and then we just have to come clean that we are lost. It's like telling yourself you don't know where you really are. Instead of facing the facts, coming to terms with that and facing it, you can sometimes blame others, or things around you and keep on to resisting the truth.

What are some of the common blind spots for sales professionals?

In your car, you're generally aware of a couple of blind spots. You check them regularly to make sure you're clearing other vehicles as you pass them, but occasionally, a blind spot still surprises you. You're driving along, as you always do, being careful (or at least thinking that you're being careful), when all of a sudden, something catches your attention from the corner of your eye and your heart stops. You narrowly avoid a crash that could have been caused by a blind spot you didn't even know existed.

Generally, we come up with plans about ways we're going to market our businesses, manage our thinking and mindset, and keep things growing and moving along smoothly, but what are we missing? Are there blind spots we don't yet know exist that could potentially be fatal to the success of our agencies? Here are three common blind spots for sales professionals:

Blind Spot #1: Giving Up Too Soon

One of the biggest mistakes I've seen real estate agents and brokers make is simply giving up too soon. We all want to chase after shiny new distractions as they show up, but many times, we already have everything we need to succeed, if we would only stay the course and allow enough time for our business ideas to take hold.

It's so important to plan for the hard times in business, (and yes, they do exist if you don't plan well) when there's very little money coming in. Plan to make smart money decisions as much as possible, both with your personal and business expenses, so that you can afford to stick with it until you start generating consistent revenue.

Many times, it's easy to look back on past ideas and failures and think, "If I had only stuck with that, I think it could have worked." You have to be willing and able to hang in there for the long haul, and so often, it's just too hard for real estate professionals to keep the momentum going.

Blind Spot #2: Not Consistently and Actively Promoting the Business

A close runner-up in fatal blind spots is not actively and consistently promoting the business. So many times, sales professionals get caught up in planning and adjusting all the minor things within the business that they neglect actually going out and finding new customers or clients on a regular basis.

I remember one of my clients who were fortunate to have gotten her start in real estate about 15 years ago. In real estate you have to work under the guidance of a broker for several years before being able to go out on your own, and one of the first things you're taught is how important lead generation is to your success. Even though my client is highly successful, I help her maintain that success, even though she is an experienced agent doing lead generation a couple of hours a day.

Part of the problem for most real estate agents is that they do not know what to specifically do when it comes to promoting their businesses. There are so many different tactics for client attraction and lead generation marketing and promotion to increase influence, impact and income that it can quickly become confusing and overwhelming. It would be far more helpful for agents to hear that they should simply pick two or three tactics for promoting their businesses, plan to stick with them for six to twelve months, and to be very aggressive with them for at least two hours each and every day. (A little free coaching here)

Blind Spot #3: Thinking You Can Do Everything Yourself

A third blind spot most agents have is thinking they can do everything themselves (or thinking that they have to do everything themselves). Lack of money, time and even experience can make an agent think he or she is not in the position to hire help, and the process of finding and building a support team can seem like a full time job on its own.

The good news is that it's possible to inch your way into delegation by finding ways to outsource one piece of your work at a time. If you don't think you can afford a paid assistant at the beginning, start with a few interns. That way, you can slowly test the waters with a support staff, while also seeing if the interns you hire would make good permanent additions to your team.

I can't tell you how many people I have guided to hire a mentor or coach first and then an assistant. Most people have that backwards. They hire the assistant, create a whole bunch of stuff, do the busy work, and later come to realize they would have saved a ton of money, energy, and time had they hired the coach or mentor first to do the right things, in the right way, and in the right order.

For most of us, the thought of starting a real estate business is as exciting as first learning to drive: we just want to be given the keys, jump in the car, and go! Certainly, there's room for the thrill of being in control and finally going where we want to go, but if we want to avoid as many fender benders as possible, it helps to know to look out for blind spots.

What blind spots do you have?

By denying the truth and by failing to face up to and own that you are out of control, you may progress towards a catastrophe. Some sales professionals fail to recognize problems and act in response to them in a timely manner because they simply don't want the problems to be true. We do not want the problems to be true, we do not want the news that sucks, and as a consequence, we become blind to the warning signs that are practically hitting us on the heads.

What are your three hard truths?

A failed attempt by an agent who hasn't got a clue how to improve her sales attraction and determines that her next marketing approach will be nothing like the first, denies to herself the possibility that the identical patterns and the same small thinking are beginning to take place in this one!

An agent or broker, proud of her standing in the community and determined to maintain the appearance of a happy and successful professional, insists to herself that all is well, even though she never remembers what she does from day to day and just operates on autopilot. By refusing to face up to the fact that you are out of control and that things are not as they should be, you let precious time creep away, and with it, precious options are lost.

A while back I had a strategy session with a potential new client. She spent a small fortune on following client attraction and lead generation home study programs, blueprints, and plans from other coaching programs and coaches. She was insistent that she followed them to a "tee" and they worked. The programs that she was modeling had created six and seven figures for other sales professionals. I called her out on using those models. If they worked so well, why didn't they work for her? She said she followed everything to the letter.

Here is what I pointed out to my new client: sales attraction and lead generation coaching programs, and coaches for that matter, come in various flavors, forms and shapes. More importantly, they come with variety of price tags. I have been privileged to have had (and continue to have) many coaches over the last several years. They have been a large part of helping me reach where I am today. It is not like I have never had my share of bad luck. I have had that experience too once or twice, but it was rare.

I do hear from many in real estate that call me up about client attraction and lead generation marketing coaching programs and other coaching that didn't produce the results they were expecting. Having coached thousands of business owners I know that there are two sides to the story. So, listening to client's stories and knowing the story from my side of the desk, I have come up with reasons why most coaching programs may not be working for you.

1. You confuse a coach to be a consultant

Client attraction and lead generation marketing consultants (at least some of them) solve problems. They are supposed to help you increase your capacity to solve problems with your client attraction marketing and mindset. If you confuse a coach to be a consultant, you will expect your problems to be solved by your coach. That will be a non-starter and for sure you won't get the results you want.

2. You are not fully committed to making the change.

There is a very clear distinction between "being interested" and "being committed." If you are being interested, you want to take action when it's convenient for you. If you are being committed, you want to take action whatever your situation.

If you are interested, then your returns on your client attraction marketing will wait for all the stars to align. If you are committed, then you will probably see the desired change with the right steps, at the right time, in the right order. If you are interested but expecting to see the results that comes from being committed, you will end up disappointed even if you are using the right steps, at the right time, and in the right order.

3. Your expectations are out of line with current reality, thinking, and mindset

Imagination has no limits and gives you the ability to understand the concept of stretching goals and going outside of your current comfort zone, thinking and mindset. However, if you "stretch too much," your expectations go out of line with reality, until you change the beliefs that block you from becoming limitless. When that happens, rarely any coach can help you. In my opinion, some sales professionals go to a coach when what they really need is a divine intervention, or a complete mindset makeover.

4. You are hiding crucial details about the current situation

Unless your coach can read your mind, he or she has only the information that you have provided to work with regarding your client attraction marketing, and mindset. You hide details and the parameters to consider while brainstorming the solution gets limited. The scope gets changed. And finally, the solution that you may come up with may be less than ideal, leading to less than ideal results.

5. You lack belief that this process will work

Henry Ford's famous quote comes in handy here – "Whether you think you can, or you think you can't – you're right."

Belief, mindset, and thinking play a major role in a coaching relationship and in coaching results. I am not suggesting you to believe blindly. That's not good in any context. But a belief in the coaching process has to be in place for you to move forward. This belief is what will set your posture right – to be in an open frame of mind as you and your coach discuss and debate options. Without that, you and your coach will both be wasting time.

Bonus Point. You forget that you still need to take ACTION to make it happen.

The sequence would typically look like this:

You or your coach identify a client attraction or lead generation marketing situation that needs change, which might include your thinking and limiting beliefs

You meet with your coach to discuss/brainstorm/debate on the issue

You both may identify potential options for moving forward

You will finally make a choice on what option to choose to proceed

You take action

Watch progress, re-adjust and refine approach as needed

Arrive at a much better situation than where you started

The part where you take action is where most drop the ball. It is where the rubber meets the road and all the resistance comes against you in full force. If you need to change a situation, you're thinking, or your mindset, that means you are expected to make some changes. Change, as we all know, is hard. So rather than taking action, you start questioning the steps before the "action step." Once you are on that path, you have a convenient excuse of "still trying to find best alternate options" before taking concrete action.

Rarely do you get any results because you have a plan.

You and your coach can come up with a plan but you still need to take action.

Your thinking and business is not too bad to fix, and it's not too late to fix it. You are an excellent woman. I want you to know that and believe that right down to your bones. Sometimes we all need to open up to our own current reality and get some help. So being truthful means taking off the rose colored goggles and seeing the world, and your business, clearly. That may mean admitting critical and immediate threats that appear on your radar screen, or identifying the slow leaks that may be draining away your hopes, and daring to dream big dreams.

Maybe the truth you must accept relates to others in your business world, but maybe the truth has more to do with you. If at this moment in your business you're living fear based, bitter, and jealous, come clean about it.

If you're scared, and don't know where to turn, be honest. If you're not, you will cheat yourself out of what may be the best opportunity you've ever had to break free of the shadows of your current business and get what you really want.

Not surprisingly, we find it much easier to see this approach at work in the businesses of other professionals.

Why can't they see how they are screwing things up?

There's a helpful example in having a fixed mindset. Almost everyone in business has the awareness of someone having a fixed mindset. You may have a fixed mindset, know of someone who does, or have had a relationship with a fixed mindset, whether it's a client, vendor, or colleague. A fixed mindset is one that is inflexible, unbending, and unwilling to change. Based on most likely knowing someone like that, how would you measure the chances of someone with a fixed mindset ever overcoming his or her limited thinking, without first facing up to the fact that a problem did in fact exist? If you put those chances at zero, you are right.

Throw Your Business Goals Out The Window

The New Successful Woman!

"The person who makes a success of living is the one who sees his goal steadily and aims for it unswervingly. That is dedication." ~ *Cecil B. DeMille*

Center your business growth goals on your values and remove your limits. The result will be you stepping out into the world as a brand new successful woman, standing out from everyone else.

When our business becomes a true expression of our values we make our greatest contributions to the world. We feel inspired, enthusiastic about growing our business, and at peace with ourselves knowing that we are fulfilling our greatest potential. The reward that comes from doing the inner work outlined in this book is the courage and, confidence to grow a business of meaning and purpose- and business growth that honors your values.

By now you should feel more empowered. You should feel centered and grounded in who you really are. Your self-confidence and self-esteem should be stronger and more abundant around growing your business. You've now integrated the essential skills to express yourself in a more powerful way. And of course, you should have started to remove your limits for what's possible for you and your business. Congratulations! Now it's time to bring this work into the world in a much bigger way.

As I mentioned before, our purpose in business is twofold. First, we need to make a commitment to our personal and spiritual growth, elevating our thoughts, words, and actions to a higher, more growth minded level. Second, we must move beyond our selfishness and contribute to others so that we leave this world a significantly better place than when we came here. Now that you've focused your energy on your inner work, it's time to orient your outer life around your values so that you can set the stage for how you will contribute your talents, and in turn become a new, wildly successful woman.
74
In this part of the book there are three areas that we'll focus on.

They are:

    1. Values

    2. Business Growth Goal Changes

    3. Action

To begin centering your business growth on your values you'll need to reconsider the work you did in earlier parts of the book to see how your values might have changed as a result of your work so far.

Next you'll have the opportunity to re-evaluate the three business growth changes you chose to make once you're clear about your non-negotiable values. Finally, with those two pieces in place, I'll show you a simple three-step process to implement these changes so you can start to center your new business growth on your values. Let's get started.

Take Action! Revisit Your Values

As you boost your inner skills by changing the way you behave in the world, it's important to re-evaluate your values. Over time your values may shift in reaction to how you evolve as situations change in your business growth and you decide to play full out. To begin the process of orienting your business around your values, take a fresh look at your four non-negotiable values and add them here.

Four non-negotiable Values:

1. _____

2. _____

3. _____

4. _____

Now that you've done that, go back and think about how your values might have changed as a result of the work you've done so far. Once you're finished considering what those might be, list your four non-negotiable values here (whether they've changed or not):

Values now:

1. _____

2. _____

3. _____

4. _____

Now that you're clear about your four non-negotiable values, the next step is to add the three business growth changes you choose to make after completing your first values exercise. To begin this process, list the business growth changes here:

Business growth changes:

1. _____

2. _____

3. _____

As you view these changes, how do you feel? Are you really stepping out and shining? Are they still the changes you need to make in order to orient your business growth around your values? If so, do they feel overwhelming? If they no longer feel right, how do they need to change to create what's really possible for you? If you choose to make the changes more challenging or to adjust them in any way, I'd also like to encourage you to take a moment to recognize how your personal growth throughout the last few parts of the book might have affected this desire. How have you grown? What qualities of character have you given a boost and improved? Are you starting to notice the new woman emerging?

When it came time for my client MaryAnn, a relationship expert and business owner, to re-evaluate her values and the business growth changes she thought she needed to make in order to honour these values, she was astonished to find that while her values had stayed the same, all of her business growth changes needed to be adapted.

Her values were:

1. Be connected
2. To feel good
3. Be generous and contribute
4. To lead

MaryAnn said she no longer felt like the business owner, and the changes she initially chose to make--change her client attraction and lead generation business strategy, end a business partnership, and go back to working with fewer clients per month--were all attempts to fill emptiness in her business. These changes had sparked a breakthrough for her that she had not counted on. Now the time and energy she was spending developing a new relationship with her had filled this emptiness.

MaryAnn's realization is a frequent one. Too often we attempt to make key business changes in reaction to something else that isn't working in our business. When we do this we set ourselves up to not succeed, choose a direction that ends up being short-term or eventually unfulfilling, and keeps us playing smaller than what is really possible for us. When you build a solid relationship with yourself you make smart business growth choices. These choices come from a deeper, more grounded place, a place that brings true and lasting fulfillment! Now feeling stronger, self-assured, and more able to stand in her own power, MaryAnn appreciated that she needed to do things in a different way. She made a decision to stay in her business partnership and continue the work in earlier parts of the book, by asking to have her needs met and by keeping her boundaries firmly in place so she could come out from behind the scenes of the team and shine in her own way.

MaryAnn also chose to keep the amount of clients that she was working with, and raised her fees to improve her finances. She understood that her energy was being drained by her debt and that handling that problem was a higher priority than working with fewer clients per month. Finally, MaryAnn also put changing her client attraction and lead generation business strategy on hold while she worked hard to get her finances in a healthier place. She realized that changing her client attraction and lead generation strategy for the sake of just making changes without a smart attraction plan was a foolish move. She needed to research and explore her options with my guidance on what works best before making such a large investment of time and money.

When MaryAnn finished re-evaluating her business growth changes they looked like this:

1. Improve my business partnership with Naomi and create a legacy that we are proud of.

2. Improve my money management, learn how to ask for the money, and get it.

3. Explore new client attraction and lead generation strategies and options using the right guidance and the right direction specifically for my bigger, bolder dreams and goals. Help more men globally understand women and their relationships while working together in business and keeping the romance in their life.

My client Deanna chose to take a different path. As a result of making a much deeper commitment to the needs of her heart she decided to step out and play in a big way. Deanna was unmarried, in her mid thirties, and now prepared to follow a lifelong dream. When she revisited her values and business growth changes she found that they were still exactly the right choices. A fitness trainer turned fitness and gym owner, Deanna had a hidden desire to train young children.

Her values were:

1.   Educate others

2.   Laughter

3.   To have fun

4.   Be fun

        To inspire

Deanna was bright and genuinely funny, and for a long time she had kept her dream of training young disabled children well hidden. After all, who would be crazy enough to give up a profitable business owning several successful gyms for a speculative business training disabled children? By clarifying her values and developing sufficient trust in her, she realized that it was time to do what she loved: Educate children about themselves and fitness using humor. Deanna chose to make her new business growth move right up to the top of her "make it happen" list. Her business growth changes looked like this:

1. Make a transition out of personally working with adults, and let her team train at the gyms.

2. Take up a career training disabled children.

3. Move from the gym and having the workouts there, to becoming mobile and working from a large bus or transport vehicle that young children would enjoy.

Deanna knew that she was taking a big risk. Many of her colleagues and team members thought she was crazy. But Deanna persevered, believing in herself and her daring big dream. Her business growth action plan looked like this:

1. Create a financial plan to support new direction.

2. Explore the bios and success stories of trainers who work with young disabled children.

3. Develop my material, specialized training, branding and positioning.

Now it's your turn to consider the business growth changes you need to make. First, make any necessary adjustments, and list your three business growth changes here:

Business Growth Changes Now:

1. _____

2. _____

3. _____

Remember to consider all aspects of your business: your clients, your business relationships, your team, your gifts and talents, your emotional, physical, and spiritual well-being, etc.
Now that you know your values and the business growth changes you'll need to honor these values, it's time to get into action. Here's an effective and productive way to make these changes, using an easy three-step process:

1. Brainstorm and come up with a plan of action

2. Expect and deal with any blocks or barriers

3. Act now

These three steps are an essential philosophy that I follow whenever I start a new undertaking or set out to make any kind of major change in my business growth.

Take Action! Brainstorm and Come Up With a Plan of Action

You may already know the exact actions you need to take to begin implementing your business growth changes. If so, then list action ideas in your journal or workbook that you have created for these goals. If not, one of the best ways to overcome blocks and determine your first steps is to call upon the wisdom of others. You can get extra help by sharing your thoughts with your colleagues and team members or hire a coach or mentor. It would be enormously helpful and they would catch your blind spots.

Because orienting your business growth around your values can feel scary, it's easy to feel blocked creatively or paralyzed by fear and anxiety. A brainstorming session with colleagues, team members or a coach will give you new ideas, great resources, and plenty of energy to get started now. When you gather the right people together for the unique purpose of generating big ideas, astonishing energy gets released and miracles start to take place.

I encourage you to have your brainstorming session in one of three ways.

1. You can invite a larger group of various professionals together to brainstorm just for you.

2. You can make it a smaller group and let everyone benefit.

3. You can hire a professional coach who excels in bigger and better thinking, who has already has helped others have a breakthrough and get help that way.

There are advantages to all of them. When I've needed bigger and better ideas, such as growing my own business in a certain specific direction, I've jumped on regular calls with my own coach and we brainstorm and implement new ideas every week. I always offer to be of support in return. I've used groups or masterminds when I've wanted to hold ongoing calls as part of a community of like-minded bigger thinking sales professionals. Years ago I belonged to a mastermind group that got together on a call once a week. That mastermind group was the catalyst for many of my successes, including my dream of becoming an author of books.

Invite a group of energetic and positive professionals to your group. Tell them you'll be brainstorming for an hour or two a week or month and invite them to bring a specific concern of their own. If you're on a team or working with a business partner, each of you should invite a couple of carefully selected people to join you.

- Keep it positive and never allow excuses for playing small in your sessions

- Eliminate lengthy discussion, long-winded stories or debate

- Keep note of all the ideas and strategies

- Keep a very open and growth oriented mindset; you never know when one silly strategy may spark a breakthrough!

Make the brainstorming session fun, yet productive. Make sure everyone benefits. Be sure each person gets some time to address his or her concerns. It's important that everyone gets an opportunity, and there's nothing more off-putting than someone who takes up all the time.

When considering potential participants, think beyond your current team to current colleagues, or business owners from your professional network. You might even consider some of the bigger players in your industry with which you do business. I've found that some of the people you'd least expect are interested, when given an opportunity to join a group of bigger and bolder growth minded sales professionals who are excited about achieving their daring big dreams and goals. You'd also be pleasantly surprised by the level of interest people have in sharing ideas and supporting the success of others.

Of course another way is just to have one-on-one power sessions as well. Each time I've conducted such sessions with a client, the level of creativity that gets expressed when we come together always astounds them. Let's look at an example of what I mean.

I met Roxanne during a workshop I attended in Los Angeles. Roxanne loved to speak. In her early fifties, she had recently recovered from a huge business loss that happened when Wall Street took a nosedive and she was now ready to make some business changes. While discussing the benefits of brainstorming, her business manager listened in as I spoke to Roxanne. Roxanne wanted some sessions because she was ready for some business growth strategies immediately.

Roxanne said she wanted to become a fulltime professional speaker who consulted with others who wanted to do the same. She loved to speak, do workshops and wanted to share this love with others, but she was concerned about her age and her ability to fit into a spotlight filled heavily with younger individuals. When she shared this with me I gave a long list of growth ideas within a short time. Here are some examples of what she got from our call:

1. Offer a class for people who would love to speak but are afraid.

2. Create a "speaking for introverts" campaign online and offline.

3. Attend local community professional group meetings and build relationships.

4. Develop a class for more mature speakers.

5. Contact several mature speakers and ask to conduct informational interviews to get some success tips and strategies.

6. Read biographies of individuals who started speaking careers later in their professions.

7. Check out speaking association websites for more information

8. Develop your own special training strategy to build confidence, courage and a unique brand and position.

9. Get re-ignited by doing something to bring back the feeling of how it felt to learn to speak.

10. Invest in your speaking talents. Start a new growth program that stretches you outside of your comfort zone.

11. Research some of the concerns that mature clients might have.

Roxanne was pleasantly surprised and energized by the suggestions and strategies. As she listened to the great ideas, her uncertainty and fear became smaller and smaller. By the end of the sessions, Roxanne was ready and raring to go. She was truly a new, successful woman.

In another session, Vanessa told me about some big dreams and goals for her business growth. She said that she wanted to combine her teaching skills with her love of travel, living the good life and working globally. She also mentioned that she loved healthy food. Here are the action steps I suggested in our session. They included:

1. Becoming an affluent travel media spokesperson and discern the best places to eat and travel.

2. Explore positions as an excursion guide for affluent clients.

3. Consider working for an international business that offers relocation services for its affluent employees.

4. Consider a position as a restaurant reviewer for an affluent travel magazine.

5. Research top end culinary schools in Europe.

6. Start your own research business for affluent business people who want to live abroad.

7. Travel writer reporting on restaurants from around the globe.

8. Become a travel writer for an international holiday and excursion company.

9. Teach abroad

10. Google and visit the library find careers that combine affluent travel and languages.

Like Roxanne, Vanessa was energized about all the big thinking business growth ideas that were creative and exciting. They both tossed out their business goals around what could not happen, and based their plans on well thought out possibilities. That's what happens when you brainstorm with others; the best of the best shines through. The excitement of realizing that anything is possible and then daring big dreams is now on the table.

Now it's your turn. Once you've completed your brainstorming session, list ten business growth action ideas here:

1. _____

2. _____

3. _____

4. _____

5. _____

6. _____

7. _____

8. _____

9. _____

10. _____

Take Action! Create Your Own Action Plan

Once you have a list of ten specific ideas or more from your brainstorming session, review them and choose five action steps. If you feel anxious about moving forward in a bigger way then you have before, it's perfectly okay to choose easy steps. If you want a strong start, choose the steps that are more challenging (these are most likely the ones you'd prefer not do). Whenever you start making specific business growth changes it's important to always put a simple action plan in place. This means choosing five items to get you started and putting them in writing to keep you on track and create momentum. Make sure they are specific and doable. As you consider which five to choose, remember this test to see if this is really big enough goals and dreams: Look for those actions that make you feel a sense of excitement and nervousness when you contemplate taking them.

When Vanessa looked over her list of ideas, she chose the following five actions to get her started:

1. Get in touch with three affluent international companies to see if they ever use traveling interpreters.

2. Research careers as an excursion guide to the affluent.

3. Google and visit the library and research careers that combine language and travel.

4. Pick up assorted affluent travel and food magazines for ideas and to see what kinds of articles combine travel and food, as well as to learn more about the writers.

What are your five actions? List them here. This list is the foundation of your action plan.

1. _____

2. _____

3. _____

4. _____

5. _____

Now you're ready for the next step:

Take Action! Expect and Deal with Any Blocks or Barriers

Before you start taking action you'll need to plan for success and achieving your goals. This means that you'll need to expect and deal with any potential blocks and barriers that might get in your way or prevent you from moving forward. As you look over your actions, ask yourself the following questions:

- What could get in my way and stop me?

- What am I really fearful of?

- What's essential for me to do to set myself up for success?

As you consider these questions write the answers in your journal or workbook. Then choose the actions you need to take to set yourself up to succeed and add them to the top of your action list.

Let's look at an example. Let's imagine that you'd like to have more time off in your business so that you can do more volunteer work in your community and belong to a large cause that you are interested in. You have your action list in place and you're ready to go. When you consider your actions you realize that two of the blocks and barriers you face are: a lack of time and fear that you may not have the necessary gifts and talent needed to be a supporter of certain causes. So, to set yourself up to succeed, you add the following actions to the top of your list:

Give up one night of just hanging around and killing time doing nothing and use this time exclusively for this improving my networking skills and speaking to new people outside of my industry.

Purchase a good product, program, or service on being supportive in large causes, and have a larger role as a supporter and volunteer to see if I have the necessary skills to take on this project.

"To achieve the impossible, one must think the absurd; to look where everyone else has looked, but to see what no else has seen." ~ Unknown

When I asked Vanessa to consider the potential blocks that might stop her from moving forward, she answered: "I'm concerned about my team. I don't know if they'll be able to handle things with me traveling for work. Also, I'll need to discuss it with my family as we are close knit and this would have an obvious effect on them." This is critical information. It's easy to see how these two potential barriers would prevent Vanessa from ever making the key changes that would honour her values and her daring big dream. Support from our team and family is critical to our success. In order for Vanessa to believe that she could in fact consider this change she'd need to add the following two action steps to the top of her list and put her two original action steps on hold:

Set up a meeting with her family to discuss my goals and travel issues.

Talk to my sisters about their availability and desire to help out with when I am away.

By dealing with these two actions first Vanessa would be increasing her chances of progressing with this process. If not, I can assure you that she'd begin to sabotage her success. Too often we ignore taking care of the pressing needs that most worry us when we think about moving forward with aligning our business growth with our values. By considering her potential blocks and barriers and building them into her action plan, she not only gave herself an advantage, she increased her motivation and excitement. Vanessa's action plan looked like this:

Set up a meeting with my family to discuss my goals and travel issues.

Talk to my sisters about their availability and desire to help out while I'm away.

Google and visit library and research careers that combine language and travel.

Read through several affluent travel and food magazines for ideas, and to research articles that might combine them.

Get in touch with two writers for informational interviews to explore the idea of freelance writing while traveling.

Take Action! Uncover Your Real Blocks and Barriers

It's important to determine the real blocks and barriers versus the perceived ones. Often we get caught up in familiar language and neglect to identify the real concern. For example, my client Joan said she wanted to work a 3-day workweek, 3 weeks a month, and still keep making her mid range six figure incomes. Joan said that her block was a fear of failure. This is a typical response. Upon hearing this, I assured her that in fact failure would be a part of her business growth experience and to realize this as part of her dream. To reveal this I asked Joan if she had ever done something that didn't come out right. "Yes," she replied, "lots of times."

"What did you do when that took place?" I asked. "I just did it again until I got it right." "Good," I said, "So you know how to deal with failure. What's really going on then? What are you really worried about?"

Joan said that her real fear was that her clients would get less benefits and results of working with her if she took more time off and they wouldn't like it if they found out about it. Once again, digging deeper, I asked if she had ever got great results for clients in the past even when she took holidays and long weekends. "Yes," she replied, "they all love working with me even more when I came back." "Well," I said, being a bit sassy, "are they from another planet? Are they somehow different from other normal business owners who would expect others to take time off and live a life of balance?" Joan laughed and, getting the idea, looked deeper for the true block.

Underneath Joan's generalized fear was a legitimate, specific concern that she did not believe that by having more time off her clients would get the same benefits and results they were now getting. As she talked about this fear she realized that we'd gotten to the root of her potential block.

Facing this truth was critical first step for Joan. Now she had something to work with. She simply needed more information. Joan decided to add "laying out a schedule" that fulfilled her needs and that of her clients to her action plan to work 3 days a week and 3 weeks a month maintain the same income working less time.

What are you really concerned about? What might be your blocks and barriers? After you think about this, take out your journal and workbook and answer the following questions:

- Are these blocks and barriers the true blocks and barriers or just a cover for something else?

- Is there something lying beneath these worries or fears?

- What's really going on? I mean really going on.

- Rewrite your real blocks and barriers here:

1. _____

2. _____

3. _____

3. _____

4. _____

Your Big Daring Dreams are Ready to Be Launched (Almost)

There are a variety of potential blocks and barriers that may stop sales professionals from taking the critical steps to orient their business growth around their values. Fear is typically at the top of the list. Since you've already begun to develop and grow your daring big dreams, this should be less of a problem. It's simple to think that the fear we feel when starting out will stay with us or, even worse, increase over time, especially when we have daring big dreams. With every positive step in the right direction, however, you become stronger and stronger. Here's another important thing to know that is rarely mentioned: excitement neutralizes fear. As you take inspired action, every success that you experience, big or small in your business, will fuel your enthusiasm to move forward, create momentum, and accomplish even more challenging goals. With this enthusiasm in place you'll move your way through challenges with more ease. For example, if you finally decide to work with a business coach, you'll probably find that your excitement about going outside of your comfort zone with something that's of interest to you will outweigh the assignments you were worried about handling in the beginning.

Sometimes fear is just a term we use for other blocks and barriers. For example, sometimes fear is just a lack of support in your business or a network of colleagues and friends who believe in you and support your business growth goals.

In the beginning, when you're making critical business growth changes, you'll need to be filled with positive support and plenty of good news. The start of any plan is the most vulnerable time, and you'll have to protect your daring big dreams by making a deliberate appeal to only hear positive feedback that strengthens your resolve. Certainly, if you do have colleagues or team members who tend to be negative, set some boundaries about what you will or will not listen to during this time of growth and change.

Don't waste your time trying to convince the Negative Nellie's or Nelson's of the viability of your plan. These people usually get energy from disagreement and their investment in why something won't work fuels the drama and crisis.

Stick with those who are big thinkers and who have your best interests at heart. With the right support in place, you'll get the energy and motivation you need to change your business. Now that you have your support in place this shouldn't be an issue.

Take Action! Get the Facts

Finally, you may recall that one of Vanessa's action steps was to contact two writers to conduct an informational interview. This is an enormously helpful step when considering any kind of business growth change. This type of interview will help you to get the facts behind the fear, explore new options, and find the best path so you can avoid the mistakes others have made. By gathering information from those who have already done what you'd like to do, whether its move to another part of the world, support large causes and become an influential volunteer, or change your job, informational interviews will help you to move forward with ease.

When you're well equipped and respectful of people's time, you'll find that most people will agree to speak with you. To be well equipped I encourage you to have questions ready before you interview someone. Here are some questions to consider:

1. If I were to think of this change as a three-stage process, what would the three stages be?

2. What kinds of skills and talents will I need to make this change?

3. Where should I invest my time and money first?

4. Where I should not invest my time and money?

5. If you had to do it all over again, what would you do differently? What mistakes might I steer clear of making?

6. What have been your main ups and downs? How might I be equipped for them?

7. Is there anyone else you recommend I speak with before start on this path?

Once you've concluded your informational interviews you now have a ton of valuable information to process and consider. Using your journal or workbook, sit down and ask yourself some questions. Questions like:

How do I feel about the information I received? Do I still want to move forward or do I have any remaining doubts?

How do I need to equip myself emotionally?

Based on what I've learned so far, is there a different area or direction I might want to consider that will have me stretch my dreams even bigger?

Do I need to speak with someone else? If so, whom?

Do I still have any blind spots that would need a mentor or coach to walk me through this process to where I want to go?

As you perform your informational interviews, be sure to note what further actions you may need to take. You'll be adding these steps to your action plan. This will help when it comes time to act.

Once you've created your action plan, worked through any expected barriers and blocks, and collected the appropriate information you might need, it's time to move forward and create some momentum.

Take Action! Get Moving!

Your values are crystal clear. You've got your specific action steps in place. You've identified any potential blocks or barriers and revised your plan. The next step is easy: Get moving. NOW! First, create an "Action Section" using the format below in your journal or workbook. You'll use this section to keep track of your progress and momentum. Next, copy your action plan into this section. Then, as you contemplate each item, put a "by when" date next to it and be sure to share this date with your partner, coach, or group. Remember that accountability and deadlines are how you create momentum.

As you act on these items, check them off or write any further information you've learned that will set you up for the next action step. For example, if you'd like to find a business coach and you get information on a search on Facebook for a business coach, write the details in the action area of your journal or workbook and update your action plan. Your new plan may include a mixture of items from your brainstorming session, or the results of what you've learned so far. With this information you're ready to create your next five action steps so you can begin to act again.

This process is simple, yet, never let the simplicity fool you. Once we figure out what needs to be done it's doing it that's usually the issue. The idea is to build in a practice of reassessing your actions and updating your plan. To do this I encourage you choose one day a week when you'll sit down, turn to the action area of your journal or workbook and assess the week's results. There should always be time scheduled in your calendar for this kind of assessment. In addition, one of the best benefits of doing this is seeing the amazing results, benefits, and outcomes of maintaining momentum. Your progress keeps you motivated to stay in action.

Make a promise to yourself to do at least one action per week. If your schedule is busy, don't let a lack of time stop you! Break down one step into smaller steps; make them bite size and doable.

When you decide to make business growth changes there is always a certain amount of fear and reluctance. Will I really succeed? Are these really the changes I need to make? Will I be sorry for my choices once I've made them? These types of questions represent the normal self-doubt that happens whenever we decide to take action to honour our values and follow our big daring dreams. Use your partner, coach, or support group to guide you through these fears. Keep in mind that once you start acting, the excitement and enthusiasm you feel will neutralize your fear and keep you motivated.

Keep this in mind: when you get stuck it's a sign that you need to ask for help. Do it often. Do it before it's beyond the point of no return. Any block or barrier can be overcome with the support of others. Also, expect to make mistakes—and lots of them. This is a lifelong process of growing and evolving over time. Be gentle with yourself. Whenever we embark on a new path it's expected that we'll get off course at given times throughout the process. Let these mistakes guide you to your next step.

Finally, when you begin to orient your business growth around your values, it is like the Universe is conspiring to help you. It's as if you step into right alignment with the Universe/God/Spirit and doors start to open.

There are clues, signs and evidence everywhere. You just need to be fully awake and pay attention- to a hunch to contact a certain agent, a surprise suggestion from a brainstorming session with a coach, or a great strategy you stumbled upon in a book. Act on these clues. They are simply the Universe/God/ Spirit opening the doors to your next step! Congratulations on the new you!

Give Voice To Your Values, And Clarify Your Vision For Success

There are countless ways of achieving greatness, but any road to achieving one's maximum potential must be built on a bedrock of respect for the individual, a commitment to excellence, and a rejection of mediocrity." ~ *Buck Rodgers*

Create a larger, more daring vision for your business and life! Start with really giving voice to your values and clarifying your vision for success. Are you ready?

Leading a business that is consistently growing and one of meaning and purpose eventually creates the craving and capacity to make a larger contribution in the world. If there's one other thing I've learned over the last eleven years, it's that there isn't anything that can top the profoundly rewarding experience of using your unique gifts to improve the world in some significant and meaningful way. Whether it's helping to end illiteracy, building a business and team to be influencers with a strong sense of integrity, wisdom and character, or treating everyone you meet with the utmost dignity, poise and grace, the role you choose to play in making the world a better place is significant.

Now, more than ever, especially with social media being used in businesses, the majority of us understand that we are each a part of a global community. Every one of us has a responsibility to stay mindful of this global connection so that we may honour the dignity of all people. As you've already learned by taking part in the exercises in this book, the most influential way to make a difference in the world is to first make a difference in your own business. By doing ALL of the work outlined in this book, you've developed the courage and confidence you'll need to not only lead a business that honors your values, but one that makes a positive impact and difference in the world. You have set in motion the unfolding of known and unknown miracles big and small to take place.

Eleven years ago my mentor asked me a question that inspired me to think beyond my individual goals toward how I might create a larger vision for my business. She said, "Beverly, as you take into account your top values and the work you'd like to do in the world, what you want for business owners that you work with?" My instant reply was, "I want them to know that they have a choice, can become the best version of themselves, and to play full out and work like they mean it."

Upon hearing my answer, she challenged me to be more exact and precise. "What do business owners need in order to know that they have choices?" she asked. "Well," I said, "They need to wake up from auto-pilot and from working and living in a robotic way so that they can feel vital, vibrant and valued. I want them to feel empowered to make choices that will allow them to work and have the business they most want to have."

Once I knew what I wanted for others, and what others needed in order to make choices in their businesses, I was prepared to look at how I might be of service. What could I offer that would help business owners all over the world feel empowered enough to make changes that would improve the quality of their businesses and therefore their lives and the lives of others? My vision for success was being clarified.

This part was easy breezy. I had constantly been a big believer in providing simple, practical tools and strategies that helped sales professionals to make manageable, doable lasting changes with joy and ease. With this in mind, I created a vision for success that continues to guide my work today:

"I champion the success of conscious, established, experienced realtors, sales professionals and small business owners, who have been in business at least 3-5 years or more so they can wake up from autopilot and contribute to their lives and work fully expressed and at their best."

When you create a larger and more daring vision for your business you intentionally make a choice to think beyond yourself. You become less concerned with personal rewards and more concerned with how others will benefit from your service, products, programs, or actions. This does not mean that you become selfless or that your needs no longer matter.

It becomes even more important that you take good care of yourself so that you're giving and serving comes from a purely intentional place- a very healthy intentional place without any attachment whatsoever to what you'll get back. This is when giving and service becomes a blessed experience for them and a by-product for you.

When you make a choice to give and be of service to others in your business, you gain the courage and confidence, and sense of rock solid determination that will fuel your work. With a daring bigger and bolder vision in place, you also become less concerned with your personal fear or self-doubt and more committed to taking the inspired actions that will support your bigger and bolder daring vision. For example, when my Realtor client Raymond lost a key team member last year, he was faced with overcoming one of his greatest fears. Losing one key member of his real estate team was devastating and Raymond was worried that it would cause some serious problems within the infrastructure of his real estate business. This was a team member who had helped to shape the business to the big success it was.

Raymond knew that in order to have peace of mind when running a real estate business, especially a small to mid-size business, you should have some sort of protection measures in place should a valued team member retire, quit, or pass away.

He worried about possible threats to the survival of the business and its financial stability that can occur. The many problems that can lead to financial instability because of the loss of a key team member include detrimental decisions made by less experienced replacements; harm to the credit rating of the business; loss of business connections; the high cost of finding, hiring, and properly training a new team member; low morale; and poor work performance of employees that remain.

A humble and a bit of an introverted real estate agent, Raymond was devastated. His business dropped and he felt disconnected to who he was and where he was going. Several months after losing a key team member, he hired someone new to take her position. Through our sessions we worked through the challenges of building and growing a business when things have gone sideways.

Raymond and I worked through a good hiring process and some of the points we decided on were:

Help clearly articulate the type of employee that will thrive in his business, on the team, and in the position. What skills was he looking for, of course, but at least as importantly: what kind of person would he like to find?

Train the people involved in the hiring process in techniques that will help gather all the information he needs during the resume review and interview stages.

Provide a system that will help him fairly and effectively evaluate candidates – and choose the best ones for his environment.

Help set up an onboard and training program that will welcome and introduce the new employee in the best possible way, and provide them with the tools and support them need to start contributing as quickly and as effectively as possible.

Making good hiring decisions, the first time, is one of the most important things a business does. We all invest tremendous amounts of time, energy, and money in the hiring processes – and if we don't, we end having to do it again and again.

Once we worked through getting the best team member, Raymond hired his dream team employee, Sandy, and things started to take off. Raymond was able to remove himself from the daily operation of his real estate business and focus more on business growth, and on growing his influence, impact and income.

Raymond was recently asked to give a speech to the people in his office about the experience of losing team members and also turning his business around and doubling his income in one year. Although Raymond had an enormous fear of publicly speaking about his business successes, he was more concerned with helping other business owners avoid all the things that had his business go sideways. His larger vision allowed him to put his fear aside.

Live What Elevates You

Take Action And Create Your
Larger More Daring Vision!

To create a larger, more daring vision for your business, you need to distinguish how you most want to improve the quality of life and business for others. This is giving voice to your values. If you could give others in the world a gift, what would you give them? If you could mend the world of some problems or difficulties, what would you mend? If you could contribute and give to others in your community, what would that contribution and giving specifically be? What do you really want for others? When considering the following questions, take your time and be specific. Use your journal or workbook to explore, brainstorm and make note of your answers.

Ask yourself:

1. What do I really want for others?

2. What do they specifically need to be able to have this?

3. How will I support, encourage and assist them in fulfilling this need?

As you think about this last question, keep your four non-negotiable values in mind. How might you use one or more of your non-negotiable values to serve your more daring vision? When you line up your values with your way or process of contribution and giving you create a powerful force for doing good in the world.

What I truly want and desire for people is

_____

Your vision may shift a little over time in your business. Never be worried about going back and refining it as needed. Then, create a powerful and personally meaningful visual or auditory reminder of this statement. You might create a vision board, collage of pictures on your desk, or a message on your computer's screensaver. Some of my clients have recorded it and play it back to themselves as they are working away on their computer. As simple as this appears, this bigger and more daring vision will help create miracles in your business and in the lives of others.

When you make a choice to invest in your inner growth as we have talked about throughout this book, you engage a bigger power than yourself to support your efforts. This same force will open many doors and opportunities for you as you set out to serve the vision you've created for your business. Once you're crystal clear about what you want for others, and you begin taking inspired actions to make it a reality, it's as if you've stepped into a flow that makes everything so much easier, better, and faster on your way to where you're meant to go.

Remember the story of Jim Carrey? His story is a perfect example of how he opened the doors to opportunities and flow when he stuck to his bigger and bolder vision. By the way, he pulled other people up with him as he became the influential and impactful star he is today.

Put Your Daring Vision Into Action

Once you've identified your bigger and bolder daring vision, it's time to put your heart and soul behind it by supporting it with your values and build an action plan. Keep in mind you don't need the perfect plan or a revolutionary or cutting edge idea, you just need to take action. Now!

To do this, choose a values-based project that will permit you to fully express and put across your vision. The size of the project doesn't really matter. For example, my client James values living and working green. When he created his vision statement, it looked like this:

"I want people to live in a clean, safe, healthy and green world."

To fulfill his vision, James created a simple project: Every new client they take on in his office (he runs several very busy spas for the owners) becomes a paperless project, all paperwork or forms are added online, and anything that is mailed has been recycled paper or products. To take it one step further James also donates 10% of all profits from each client to Habitat for Humanity.

Habitat for Humanity is a national, non-profit organization working towards a world where everyone has a safe and decent place to live. This is his way of contributing to a cleaner, safer environment. His clients are aware of this project and when they work with him know that he is donating towards this type of cause. This kind of thinking has clients work with and refer James because they love who he is, and how he works from a bigger dream. The best part is James works for others, who own the spas, and his big dream is to open his own chain, and on the last call we had, we upped the time frame for him to do that. Very exciting.

Take Action! Create a Values-Based Project

As you go over your vision statement think about the inspired actions you'd like to take to fulfill your vision. If you're not sure what to do, ask your business partner, colleagues or coach for help with ideas and strategies.

Share your vision statement and your non-negotiable values with them. You might even hold a brainstorming session to get a variety of ideas.

Here's how to get started:

1. Choose a specific project.

2. Give your project a name.

3. Use the three-step process from part seven to create a plan for action. The three steps are:

Brainstorm and come up with a plan of action.

Expect and deal with any blocks or barriers.

Act now

Start with small steps that are bite size and doable. Never worry about doing things absolutely perfectly, just focus on taking action. Whether your dream is to have vision as large as Oprah's, Jim's, James, Rebecca, or MaryAnn's, you get to decide.

Whether you choose to become a star in your own right, implement a green program in your business and help others live in safe and clean community, or start a foundation, your contribution, giving, and service is important. Get started on your own project today!

Support and Reinforce the Success of Others

There is another great way you can serve and give to the greater good of the world with the skill you've learned: support and reinforce the success of others. Now that you've become awakened and aware of how important it is to express your power and dare to dream really big dreams, helping others do the same is a vital next step.

For example, you might gently challenge your clients or colleagues to stop playing small and hiding out, or inspire a team member to pursue an important dream of their own.

Helping Others Succeed – Learn a Lesson from Oprah

With the ending of The Oprah Winfrey Show a lot of attention has been placed on Oprah - her success, what she's doing next and of course, tons of memories.

There is certainly a lot to learn from Oprah about how to be successful and as we all know, how she helped others.

There was once a leader who recognized her talent and helped her. And I'd like for you to consider what kind of a leader are you in your business. Everyone has natural talents that can propel their success as we have talked about in this book. However, most people meet leaders who set up roadblocks to success rather clear the highway for others success.

The CBS Early Show did a segment called The Man Who Discovered Oprah, Dennis Swanson. I encourage you to read the article or watch the video. There is one very important observation I would like to make:

He asked Oprah to be herself. No changes.

He could have asked her to lose weight, change her look, and change her style. Those are examples of typical success roadblock that leaders put up. "Do it this way" rather than what comes natural to you. Instead, he said "be you" and helped her get what she needed to be successful.

What is the result? Oprah developed the confidence in her and in her natural abilities and style. Oprah is arguably one of the most genuine people on TV, or in all of business for that matter. You get to see her at her best and worst, and people love her for it. It's made her one of the richest and most influential people alive. Throughout her career she could have sat back and just lived off what she made. Instead, right from the beginning she supported and reinforced the success of others.

As a leader what are you doing to help your team be the best by being who they are? Your business may not catapult someone to stardom like Oprah, but it may catapult them to extreme success in another way. And by now, have you figured out that when you help others that it is improving your bottom line as well? Take Oprah's show for instance. Every week for 25 years she helped people in big and small ways. Do you think it improved her bottom line, her bank account, indirectly as a result of giving and serving?

Personal branding is an important part of this lesson as well. Oprah understood who she was, her personal brand. Dennis Swanson also understood her personal brand and helped her create an environment for her brand to be brought to life. And, as she grew her business, her giving got bigger and bigger and bigger. But then again so did her bank account.

Are you a roadblock or are you clearing the highway for the success of people you know in your business? When you understand that helping others helps your bottom line, it can be one of the most life changing gifts that you can ever give yourself.

Here are some of the things you can do to become more of an impactful influencer to help others achieve their bigger and bolder daring dreams:

> - Offer your help and lend a helping hand. Support and encourage the dreams and goals of others by offering to participate in a brainstorming session or by providing helpful resources.

- Look for and find what works. When a client, team member, or colleague has the courage to share a dream or desire, highlight the strengths of their plan and the qualities they possess that will allow them to make it a reality. Avoid sharing any criticism, disapproval or negativity. Laser focus on what works instead of focusing on potential blocks and barriers.

- Do away with being sarcastic, ridiculing, and teasing. Learn to look for and recognize the strengths and talents of others.

- Refuse to participate in gossip or slandering of any sort.

- Shift your conversations from struggles to success. Talk about what's working in your business and encourage others to do the same.

- Join a mastermind group or hire a coach.

- Mentor an up-and-coming colleague, realtor, mortgage broker or team member.

Your support and your supporters will come from the most amazing places and in the most amazing ways.

I still remember hearing this in a Michael Buble interview and the story has stuck with me. For those of you who don't know who Michael is, he is a Canadian singer and actor. He has won several awards, including three Grammy Awards and multiple Juno Awards.

Michael Buble credits his plumber grandfather for his big break. His grandfather would land the young crooner club shows in and around his native Vancouver, British Columbia in return for free pipe maintenance.

The singer would craft his vocal skills while fishing with his father and then his impressed granddad - a big fan of the standards and performers like Frank Sinatra and Tony Bennett - would work as his makeshift manager.

Buble recalls, "He took me to every audition. He took me to every singing lesson. He would get me in by promising to give free plumbing to any club owner who would let me in. He'd say, 'Listen, I know he's 16 but you let him up onstage and I'm gonna go and fix your hot water heater. It's busted.' Then he'd wait all night and I'd have my chance to sing with the band and he sat there beaming at me."

Grandpa would also join the young star for early morning shopping mall sessions at Christmas, when Buble would belt out festive tunes for hours.

He adds, "He'd drink about eight cups of coffee, the poor guy... and we'd sit there for five hours."

But all the effort paid off a week after Buble met with Warner Brothers Music officials in Los Angeles and begged them to take him and his music seriously.

He tells TV news show 60 Minutes, "I was down in the basement of this building that I was staying in and I was on the treadmill and the doors flung open and my grandfather and my manager were there and they both had tears in their eyes and my grandfather said, 'Sunshine, you're with Warner Brothers.'"

You can see the positive influence that Michael's grandfather had on his life and future business success. You can have that kind of influence on someone's life too. Now that you know everything you say and do could have an enormous impact on the future of someone close to you, how will you behave, serve or give differently?

Take Action! Lift Someone Up

Make a conscious decision to support and encourage at least one person. Choose that person and write his or her name here:

_____

Next, how will you specifically support and encourage this person? List three specific examples of what you can do here, and put a date by when you will do each one. Also, make note of it on your calendar!

1. _____

2. _____

3. _____

　　　　Spend a little more time with a client who could use your help on a challenging project. Make a point to acknowledge the strength of a team member or even your competition on a regular basis. You might simply become a friendly face on Facebook who drops by someone's page and leaves some helpful content without selling anything. While I know that most of us are busy growing our businesses, let's remember what really matters- our connection and engagement with one another.

Leave Your Legacy
and Help More People

The steps outlined in this book involve an ongoing process of change and then creating momentum with those changes. The work that this book contains never ends, and the numerous rewards, big and small, won't either. I can guarantee you will be challenged to use these skills on a whole big new level with each stage of growth you experience in your business. When you need a reminder that you have what it takes to lead your business growth, remember the following:

1. Become the best version of you. Invest in an ongoing relationship with yourself by staying fully connected to your inner game. Dare something big.

2. Come out of hiding, stop playing small, and shine. Let your thoughts, words, and actions express your true essence-the very best version of who you REALLY are. Laugh more and play more.

3. Negative people are rarely content. Strengthen relationships by being discerning about where you spend your time, who you follow, or who you choose to work with. Improve the relationship with yourself to become indispensable to others.

4. Build your courage and confidence. Look fear in the eyeball and use challenging situations to make yourself even stronger and more powerful.

5. Work through your unfinished stuff. Keep your spiritual strength, emotional health, and standards high so you won't undersell your needs and desire to dare to dream big dreams. You are an excellent woman, and we all need help from time to time.

6. Honor your values by making smart choices and decisions that keep your business centered on what matters most in the short term and long term.

7. Link your business goals and daring dreams to a larger vision that enables you to truly make a difference in the world. Give voice to your values, and clarify your vision.

As you continue to use and maintain these skills you will experience much more joy and deep contentment that comes from fulfilling your daring big dreams and goals- the mission that allows you to express your greatest potential while becoming the best version of yourself. Your commitment and dedication to becoming the best version of yourself will give you the courage, confidence and cojones to leave a legacy that makes this world a much-improved place for those who follow after you. Your contribution and involvement is extremely vital.

As you encourage and support the success of others, you'll arrive at the end of your business life knowing that your presence made a difference. There is nothing greater than lifting up others. Your ability to leave a powerful and lasting legacy rests on your commitment and dedication to this inner work- the work that will allow you to dare to dream big dreams and help others fulfill theirs too!

ABOUT THE AUTHOR

Beverly Boston
North America's #1 Real Estate, Sales Coach and Mentor

Four Seasons Hotels, UBC, Labinal, Masco, Bank of America, Royal Bank, Dominion Lending, REMAX, Coldwell Banker, Prudential, Century 21 Weichert, MacDonald, Sutton, Sotheby's, Keller Williams, Long & Foster, Royal LePage, Dexter, and many more think of me as an expert in the big arena for smart real estate and sales professionals-the real business world.

With over 17,000 hours of coaching, training, and mentoring as well as 3 decades of study and researchinto what makes real estate and sales professionals successful–I keep it real and relevant.

I help sales professionals, realtors, and mortgage brokers obtain freedom from being stuck & broke in a self-employed mindset, to an executive mindset by delegating, automating and replicating systems to building an empire with a visionary and luminary outlook and make meaningful change in the world. One of my clients increased her income by 10.6 times over in just a few months

FREE BONUSES

KICK-START REAL CHANGE AND GROWTH TODAY!

How do smart real estate and sales professionals think and grow rich while making a difference?

Smart people take action.

Get started today, by downloading Beverly's popular *Business Breakthroughs Ki*t. This popular kit includes FREE access to her award-winning Breakthroughs Assessment, Breakthroughs Dynamic ebook and the Smart People's Achievement Formula.

http://beverlyboston.com/actnow